T0382782

Inflation, Income Distribution and X-Efficiency Theory

First published in 1980, *Inflation, Income Distribution and X-Efficiency Theory* presents an exploratory theoretical study of the linkages between income distribution, the degree of X-efficiency, and inflation and the level of employment in the context of developing society. It discusses themes like concept of income distribution; maximization versus non-maximization models; theory of inert areas; microtheory and inflation; monopoly and X-Efficiency theory; contracts, bargaining and inflation; theory of bargaining; survival strategies in the face of inflation; and policy implications of inflation. This book is a must read for students and scholars of macroeconomics and economics in general.

Inflation, Income Distribution and X-Efficiency Theory

A Study Prepared for the International Labour Office...

Harvey Leibenstein

Routledge
Taylor & Francis Group

First published in 1980
by Croom Helm

This edition first published in 2022 by Routledge
4 Park Square, Milton Park, Abingdon, Oxon, OX14 4RN

and by Routledge
605 Third Avenue, New York, NY 10017

Routledge is an imprint of the Taylor & Francis Group, an informa business

Publisher's Note
The publisher has gone to great lengths to ensure the quality of this reprint but points
out that some imperfections in the original copies may be apparent.

Disclaimer
The publisher has made every effort to trace copyright holders and welcomes
correspondence from those they have been unable to contact.

A Library of Congress record exists under ISBN: 0709903065

ISBN: 978-1-032-32167-7 (hbk)
ISBN: 978-1-003-31320-5 (ebk)
ISBN: 978-1-032-32172-1 (pbk)

Book DOI 10.4324/9781003313205

Inflation, Income Distribution and X-Efficiency Theory

A study prepared for the International Labour Office
within the framework of the World Employment Programme

Harvey Leibenstein

CROOM HELM LONDON

BARNES & NOBLE BOOKS NEW YORK

(a division of Harper & Row Publishers, Inc.)

© 1980 International Labour Organisation
Croom Helm Ltd, 2-10 St John's Road, London SW11

British Library Cataloguing in Publication Data

Leibenstein, Harvey
    Inflation, income distribution and x-efficiency
    theory.
    1. Underdeveloped areas – Income distribution
    2. Underdeveloped areas – Inflation
    I. Title II. International Labor Organisation.
    World Employment Programme
    339.2'09172'4   HC59.7
    ISBN 0-7099-0306-5

Published in the USA 1980 by
Harper & Row Publishers, Inc.
Barnes & Noble Import Division
Library of Congress Cataloging Card Number: 79-57323

ISBN 0–06–494169–8

Typeset by Leaper & Gard Ltd, Bristol

Reproduced from copy supplied
printed and bound in Great Britain
by Billing and Sons Limited
Guildford, London, Oxford, Worcester

CONTENTS

1 INTRODUCTION

In the course of doing this study I was surprised to discover that there existed virtually no systematic work on the consequences of inflation on the development of less developed countries — and especially on the impact of inflation on income distribution. What is meant by systematic is specified in later chapters, but one does not have to interpret this term too narrowly to learn that it is difficult to find anything even in relatively well-stocked economics libraries. Also, the relation of bargaining power to the impact of inflation on income distribution is rarely, if ever, treated in studies of income distribution in less developed countries. I hope that readers of this book will be convinced, as I am, that connecting bargaining power to income distribution is a natural way of looking at the problem.

Inflation has to be studied from a special viewpoint, one that differs from that of conventional microeconomic theory, if we are to see the role that bargaining power plays in determining the impact of inflation on income distribution and development. These basic ideas represent the viewpoint that is expounded in Chapters 3 and 4 under the rubric of X-efficiency theory. These ideas are too complex to be captured in a paragraph or two, but are quite straightforward when considered in the course of a chapter or two. For readers who are economists one bit of special mental effort may be required. We have to forget the postulate of maximising behaviour, or be ready to relax that assumption at various points in our discussion.

In the last three decades the economic experiences of most developing countries have been accompanied by various degrees of inflation. Surprisingly, inflation has not been a central subject of study within the economic development literature. Nor for that matter, has it been a central issue in the examination of the determinants and consequences of income distribution. There are probably a number of institutional reasons for the way economists choose subjects for study which may help explain why this should be the case. One additional aspect comes to mind: existing economic theory does not readily lend itself to connecting inflation and those phenomena having to do with employment, productivity, innovation and capital accumulation, which are central elements in the study of economic development.

For the most part inflation has been viewed by economists as a macroeconomic phenomenon. According to this view, inflation is something which is caused by, and should be understood in terms of, governmental economic activities. On the one hand, inflation is most frequently seen as a consequence of central bank policies and its influence on the aggregate supply of money, the interest rate and the supply credit. Equally important is the view of inflation as a consequence of government taxation and expenditure policies. Since, in the course of development, governments frequently face considerable pressure to increase expenditures beyond their actual tax receipts, or even beyond their taxing powers, governments yield to deficit finance policies. There can be little doubt that the handling of the monetary and budgetary aspects of government are extremely significant elements in our understanding of the inflation process. Nevertheless, it is only part of the overall picture.

It is myopic to see inflation only as a macro phenomenon and to miss or understate micro elements. This is similar to viewing price determination by looking only at the supply side without examining the demand side; and, in part, it is similar to looking at aggregates without examining in any way the individual decisions and acts which are the components of the summarised statements which express aggregate behaviour.

For a moment let us look at inflation from a simple viewpoint; namely, as an increase in the average prices of goods and services. It is incorrect to believe that governments are the only ones that determine the price level. Prices are set by firms, and by those who engage in producing goods and services and trading in them. Thus, the way in which prices are set is either part of the market mechanism, or part of the administrative mechanisms used by private or public firms. These mechanisms and bargaining procedures cannot be ignored if we are to understand the inflationary process. This brings us to the analysis of the relation between price setting and the forces that determine prices in specific individual markets. Two aspects come to mind on the nature of these forces: (i) those elements that determine the nature of the bargains made within markets, and (ii) the changing costs of production and distribution. The latter involves the productivity of labour when labour is viewed in the broadest possible sense. The former involves the nature of markets which we will discuss later in terms of the concept of relative bargaining power.

Why should we care about either bargaining power or productivity in the analysis of inflation? We will argue that both help to determine two significant aspects of inflation: the generation of inflationary pressure which increases the demand for money, and the impact of inflation on income distribution.

It may be argued that the impact of inflation on income distribution is a short-run phenomenon — that somehow it all evens out in the long run and that income distribution is determined by 'real' factors, such as relative input productivity, and the distribution of ownership of inputs. Even if this were the case, it is nevertheless important to examine whether we should care about short-run influences on income distribution. We will show that this is especially significant with respect to welfare criteria that we shall introduce as a way of assessing the importance of different income distributions. Most important, this welfare criterion, the 'vulnerability criterion', is especially significant in the case of developing countries.

Inflationary processes distort various prices and related

elements in the economy, and distort the normal incentives which influence economic behaviour. This is especially likely to be important in the case of developing countries, since such effects of inflation on production, and on the specific nature of capital accumulated, are likely to determine the degree of employment creation. To the extent that developing countries are characterised by various degrees of open and disguised urban employment, we will want to study the extent to which such aspects are influenced by the same considerations which influence the building up of inflationary pressures, and its detailed impact on the distribution of income.

In the course of carrying out the study, it became apparent to the author that a good deal of the statistical basis for the study of such problems simply does not exist. In part this may be that statistics have not been collected for other purposes. For example, international trade statistics are frequently collected as a consequence of the administration of a system of tariffs and import licences. But, with respect to the issues we are considering, especially the relationship between inflation and production, there is little reason for us to collect such statistics as a by-product of other administrative duties. In addition, the sort of questions we raise in this study simply have not been asked, or not asked forcefully enough, so that there has been no intelligent reason, or policy purposes for collecting statistics of the type desired. In general, then, there have been both theoretical and practical reasons why the kind of questions we will want to consider can not be handled at the present on a solid empirical basis. Nevertheless, part of the objective of this study is to argue that these questions are significant.

This book should be viewed as an exploratory theoretical study. It is essentially a speculative essay on a number of issues that are usually not connected to each other, but which we plan to link in various ways, in the hope that the material will suggest that such linkages are useful. Our major aim is to see if reasonable links can be established between such aspects of an economy as its income distribution, the degree of X-efficiency, inflation and the level of employment in the context of a developing society, and to see if any interesting implications result. Not all possible linkages will be attempted, and special efforts will be made not to attempt to forge links artificially.

The basic linkages to be emphasised are the following: (i) to show that there are connections between X-efficiency theory and the process of inflation, apart from the inflation dampening influences of governmental monetary and budgetary policies; (ii) to some extent, we hope to examine the impact of inflation on some characteristics or components of income distribution; (iii) also, an attempt will be made to relate the inflation process to the determination of the level of employment. Thus, the basic links will be between X-efficiency theory, inflation and employment creation; (iv) finally, the policy implications of these various linkages will be taken up in the last chapter.

2 ON INCOME DISTRIBUTION

I. Income Distribution – Some General Remarks

Both as a field of research, and as an area of practical concern, work in income distribution is exceedingly diffuse. There is an unusually large number of specific topics that comes under this heading. While this is hardly the place to review the entire field,[1] it may be useful to make some general remarks to separate those aspects we will consider, or touch on, from those which we will ignore.

One curious characteristic of the field is that most of the statistical literature appears to be almost completely unrelated to the theoretical work done in this area. For example, most statistical work has to do with the size distribution of incomes. In particular, a number of inequality coefficients have been developed and computed, such as the Gini coefficient, whose intent is to indicate the degree of inequality of a specific income distribution, or to compare degrees of inequalities of different income distributions.[2] Yet, as has been argued by Chenery,[3] as well as others, we have no theory for size distribution of income. On the other hand, most of the theoretical work that does exist deals with the functional theory of income distribution. On a macro level, it involves the theory of specific wage rates earned by individuals with specific skills. The neoclassical marginal productivity theory of labour is the major example of this type. Both a theory of functional shares between those that provide labour and those that provide capital, and the specific wage theory, depends on the notion of the production function. In fact, all of these theories are connected in some way via the theory of production, and loosely connected to the theory of size distribution, but the connection is incomplete.

Consider for a moment the theory of wages and its possible

12

connection to the size distribution of income. Clearly, the wages received by individuals are related to income distribution, but they are only a part of the factors that determine income distribution. At the very least, we would also need a theory of asset ownership and its distribution, in order to explain income distribution. But we do not have a theory of the distribution of asset ownership.[4] This is entirely apart from the question as to whether or not any particular theory of wages happens to be correct. While some of the considerations concerning the theory of wages, and its applicability to income distribution problems, apply to all economics, there is one set of considerations that is especially applicable to the less developed countries. Even if we had a theory of wages that was an adequate theory for income distribution explanations, it would only apply to wage-receiving labour. But one of the characteristics of less developed countries is that a very high proportion of those generally designated as the poor are self-employed. Most frequently they are self-employed in what has been termed the informal market. The magnitude of those who are self-employed is frequently over fifty per cent, among the poorest portion of the people. Hence, even if wage theory did apply to those who are employees, it would be unhelpful in examining the income received by the self-employed and, hence, would be unhelpful in understanding the most vulnerable portion within the income distribution.[5] The two other elements which are exceedingly important are the family, through the inheritance system, which in part influences the distribution of assets, and the family's role in determining education, which in turn influences the distribution of skills.[6] It seems quite obvious that in many instances, family position is one of the main factors in determining an individual's position in the income distribution. Hence, demographic variables turn out, in various ways, to be exceedingly important as forces that determine income distribution.

An interesting speculation on these matters, which connects some of the factors we have discussed to problems of economic development, is presented in the study by Adelman and Morris. They write:

> Our analysis provides some grounds for speculating about the mechanisms that operate before the takeoff point to depress the standard of living of the poorest 40 per cent. In the very earliest stage of dualistic growth, increased wage payments to indigenous workers in modern plantation, extractive, and industrial enterprises tend to be more than offset by concurrent changes in population, relative prices tastes, and product availability. The lowering of death rates through the introduction of modern health measures such as malaria control accelerates population growth and thus tends to depress the per capita income of the indigenous population. Since cash wages are not immediately matched by increased availability of consumer's goods, higher prices erode gains in money income. Subsistence farmers shifting to cash crops are particularly hard hit by rising prices. Typically they suffer both declines in real income and nutritional deficiencies as they become dependent on the market for major necessities previously produced at home.[7]

The view presented by Adelman and Morris is of special interest, since it is based on a great deal of cross-sectional statistical work involving 74 countries and employing 48 qualitative measures of social, economic, and political variables.

Adelman's and Morris's concern with the lowest 40 per cent in the income distribution, brings up another aspect of the literature. A great many writers are really concerned with the sources of poverty, or relative poverty, rather than with income distribution as such. There is a special concern with more impoverished segments of society and attempts to explain how their condition fluctuates in the course of economic development. This concern should be kept in mind in the next section, in connection with our discussion of the concept of 'vulnerability'.

The causation of relative poverty may run for various circumstances to poverty, but a more heroic hypothesis that is sometimes invoked, is that there is a clear-cut relationship between economic development and relative poverty. On the whole, a number of authorities agree that, in general, the income distribution worsens in the early stages of development, but that it improves as development proceeds.[8] Whether this is factually true, or whether it is an artefact of the extreme data problems involved in measuring real income in the agricultural sector, is difficult to determine. It should be mentioned in passing that most relatively careful studies indicate considerable concern about the quality of income distribution data, but, despite this concern, the writers usually proceed in the attempt to measure degrees of inequality to the best of their ability.

In this book we shall simultaneously be concerned with the income distribution problem in terms of the functional distribution of income, as well as those aspects that deal with the relatively impoverished members of society. The reason for this dual concern is not because we feel there is a clear-cut relationship between the functional distribution and the lower deciles of the size distribution, but because the main analytical ideas which we shall employ happen to have considerable bearing on the production function, and theories which explain the functional distribution on that basis, as well as a bearing on some aspects of the size distribution of income.

To the extent possible, we will attempt to avoid judgements on the problem of income distribution as such. The main reason for this is not that it is necessarily desirable to avoid such judgements, but simply that to do so would involve a variety of philosophical issues that would detract from the type of considerations that are the main point of this book.

II. Comments on the Concept of Income Distribution

Income inequality is a complex and subtle idea which looks
as though it is a simple one. The main reason it is frequently
considered simple is because it often seems easy for people to
make comparisons. Thus it is easy for some individual to
argue that another individual is much richer than he is, or
appears to be. Even this statement, on further reflection, is
far from simple if we take life cycles into account. Once we
introduce a multiplicity of individuals, the complexity becomes much more readily apparent.[9]

To see the nature of some of the difficulties it may be of
interest to examine a variety of circumstances under which it
appears that individuals are economically equal, but where
from some viewpoints they actually do not appear to be so.
In other words, we consider a number of situations in which
it becomes difficult to determine whether equality or inequality exists.

The first situation in which everyone appears to be equal,
is one in which all those who receive an income, receive precisely the same monetary income. This represents equality
even if the individuals are *not* the same age, have different
capacities, contribute differently to the economy, and have
in some sense that from a purely arithmetic viewpoint everyone has a paycheck which has the same numbers on it.

Now consider a second situation in which economic equality may be said to exist. Suppose that all working individuals
receive the same age-income profile. In other words, we
visualise that for every individual there is a similar career
pattern in terms of their income, that they all start working
at the same age, and that for any given age, every individual
receives the same income. However, as an individual gets
older his income increases up to some point beyond which it
either flattens or declines. Such age-income profiles may
be justified on a variety of grounds, such as learning from
experience, or increased productivity as a consequence of
experience, or increased need with age, etc. The reason

behind a rising age-income profile need not concern us at this stage. The point to be observed is that there is a sense in which everyone receives the same income over his or her lifetime. However, at any point in time, since different individuals will be at different ages, the income distribution will not be equal. Does this represent an equal or an unequal income distribution?

Or, consider the case in which the age distribution of the population changes. Suppose that in the situation we have just described the birth rate falls and, as a consequence, the population becomes older on the average. As a result, there is a somewhat larger proportion in the older age groups. The initial appearance of this effect will be an apparent decrease in the inequality of income. But does such an apparent decrease have any significant economic impact if everyone is receiving an income consistent with the age-income profile? To the extent that age distributions are not taken into account in existing attempts to measure the concentration of income, through such criteria as the Gini distribution, such attempts may mostly reflect age distribution changes rather than actual income inequality changes. In any event, it seems clear that the criteria of everyone receiving the same age-income profile, as against the same income at a point in time, readily conflict with each other, although there is a sense in which they represent income distributions which are equal.

Let us now consider one more example in the spirit of those considered above. Suppose we consider an agrarian economy in which each household occupies a piece of land of equal size and of equal fertility. There is a sense, in this case, in which it can be said that everyone is in the same economic circumstances. However, the output from the land will depend on the amount of effort put into it by those who work the land. Suppose some farmers prefer more leisure than others, and are willing to trade off some of the food they grow for an increase in leisure. There may be a sense in which it can be said that those who choose a more food-less leisure bundle feel just as well off as those who choose less food and more leisure. Nevertheless, in terms of income as usually measured, it can be argued that those who grow less farm produce have a smaller income than those who grow more.

Another example which creates similar difficulties, is to suppose that every individual in our agrarian economy (or for that matter, in any economy) has the same output, but the family sizes of different households differ. Thus the production value of working households is the same, but their consumption differs since in larger households members have to share their income with, let us say, more non-working members. Once again there is a sense in which this represents equality and a sense in which it represents inequality. A slightly different but important variant on the above example is the situation in which those who work have equal income, but unequal responsibilities for the partial maintenance of others in an extended family system. It is quite immaterial whether undertaking such responsibilities is voluntary or not. Those who choose to undertake such responsibilities voluntarily will have a lower consumption level than those who choose not to. Once again incomes are equal but consumption levels are not. There are those who might argue that as long as the incomes are equal, the fact that some choose to be charitable to others does not affect the situation, and, hence, we should look at this as a case of real income equality. But suppose that, in this case, individuals feel that their responsibilities to members of their extended families are not really voluntary, but are mandatory in terms of the culture in which they live. One might say that this is similar to cases in which the extended family imposes a 'tax' on those who work, for the maintenance of those who, for a variety of reasons, do not work. The question which arises is whether we should consider the income before or after 'taxes'. If equality implies income after taxes, then of course the felt mandatory responsibilities change the situation and incomes should be viewed as unequal.

There are variations on the above, which will be mentioned

only briefly. In the case of developing economies which are of a dualistic nature, it is important not only to consider the usually lower money income from the rural sector, but also the possible cost-of-living differences, and the nature and capabilities to measure the non-monetised sector. In a sense this involves something similar to the effort-leisure problem considered above, since, in that example, leisure is part of the non-monetised sector. Even if family incomes are the same in different households, there may be a different way of distributing the family income. Should such income distributions be taken into account in assessing whether equality, or a lack of equality, exists?

One reason for considering the various complexities in the previous paragraph is simply that the meaning of income inequality, and, hence, the meaning of changes in degrees of equality, is an inescapable part of the problem of examining the impact of inflation on income distribution. Clearly there are some difficult definitional problems involved. An aspect that we want to consider is whether we can avoid some of the difficulties if we choose as our criterion the degree of *vulnerability* to various disabilities that a worsening of the income distribution may impose on some individuals. What we have in mind by this concept is that certain non-continuous influences may be involved as a consequence of low income. For example, consider the matter of the consumption of calories. At some very low income, a sustained low-calorie consumption level may lead to specific vulnerabilities to various types of diseases, or to differences in the ability to carry out normal work, etc. Without going into all possible examples and details, suffice it to say that there is a nutritional sense in which people do appear to have certain minimal, targeted needs in order to carry out various activities. This is usually stated as minimum target values. However, one of the effects of a worsening of the income distribution may be to put a higher proportion of the population below some given target value, determined on nutritional or other biological grounds, which may be readily measurable. Thus, one reason why we should care about the impact of an income distribution is because this will in turn have an impact on portions of the population vulnerable to disease, or other predetermined disabilities.

With respect to the problem of inflation, *vulnerability* may be an especially interesting concern. In general it is expected that inflation will frequently hit some highly vulnerable groups, such as pensioners, whose nominal incomes are fixed, or holders of assets (e.g. lifetime savings for emergencies or old age security), denominated in nominal terms. However, even if we consider the case in which all incomes are adjusted in the long-run inflation losses, there may still be a vulnerability concern. In an inflationary period not everyone can have his income or value of assets adjusted immediately. In the short run, contractual arrangements and unbalanced bargaining capacities result in differential lags before contracts and obligations can be re-adjusted. Thus in 'short-run' periods, some lose before they get their chance to catch-up. For some of the short-run losers, their degree of vulnerability may be a serious concern.

Notes

1. For an excellent review of the literature in this area see Felix Paukert, *International Labour Review*, vol. 108, nos. 2-3 (August-September 1973).

2. A thorough comparison of the most prominent measures of inequality that have traditionally been utilised in the study of income distribution can be found in Richard Weisskoff, 'Income Distribution and Economic Growth in Puerto Rico, Argentina, and Mexico', *Review of Income and Wealth*, vol. 16 (December), pp. 305-9; and Amartya Sen, *On Economic Inequality* (Oxford University Press, London, 1973), pp. 24-46.

It would be useful to recapitulate an important caveat on the use of the various measures of inequality given by Weisskoff, 'It must be emphasized that these measures of inequality and the income shares cannot be used to indicate whether the "poor are getting poorer" or the "rich are getting richer" in real terms. At best, the detailed income shares do indicate whether segments of the distribution have gained or lost relative to other segments. For example, the share of income received by the bottom 10 percent of families in a given county may fall from 6 percent to 4 percent, but the absolute level of income of those families may be doubling at the same time' (p. 309).

3. 'Existing theories of income distribution are of only limited value in establishing an analytical framework for comprehensive governmental action because they are somewhat narrowly focused on the functional distribution of income between labor and capital', Hollis B. Chenery *et al., Redistribution with Growth* (Oxford University Press, London, 1974), p. 43.

4. There is considerable evidence that the distributon of assets is more concentrated than the distribution of incomes. According to Chenery *et al.,* 'Whatever the shares of labor and capital as determined in the factor markets, greater equality of personal incomes could be achieved if ownership of private capital and access to public facilities were more equally distributed', *Redistribution with Growth*, p. 44.

5. Chenery *et al., Redistribution with Growth*, p. 23.

6. A similar point was made by Fishlow: '. . . families, while an important mechanism for redistribution of income at a moment of time, also are an important source for transmitting inequality into the future. To the extent that the probability of children earning increased income in the future is influenced by parents' income, equality of opportunity will not prevail, and inequality will tend to persist'. Further, 'children carry with them not only the scars of malnutrition, no transference of past assets and status, and limited aspirations, but also deprivation of education'. See Albert Fishlow, 'Brazilian Size Distribution of Income', *American Economic Review*, vol. 62 (May), pp. 392 and 395.

7. Irma Adelman and Cynthia Taft Morris, *Economic Growth and Social Equity in Developing Countries* (Stanford University Press, Stanford, 1973), p. 181.

8. For a current discussion of the relationship between economic development and the distribution of income, see Chenery *et al., Redistribution with Growth*, p. 17.

9. Simon Kuznets, 'Economic Growth and Income Inequality', *American Economic Review*, vol. 45 (March 1955), pp. 1-3.

3 X-EFFICIENCY THEORY[1]

I. Maximisation Versus Non-maximisation Models

In conventional microeconomic analysis, maximisation and optimisation ideas underlie the modes of thought involved. Since the theory presented in this book will be based on significant departures from the postulate of maximising behaviour, it may be useful to consider briefly at the outset the maximisation postulate and possible alternatives. This is especially important, since maximisation under constraint is not only the basic notion that dominates microeconomic theory, but also permeates many aspects of applied economics. For example, in some of the recent work on the economic theory of human fertility,[2] the concept of maximising utility under constraint is utilised to explain the fertility behaviour of households. In other areas of applied work in which an equation system is postulated at the outset, the analysis frequently proceeds on the basis of maximisation, in the sense that investigators will frequently attempt to derive the outcome from the initial equations and from the parameters that have been established empirically, which in turn depends on an implicit or explicit maximisation assumption.

In other words, the investigator will obtain his results by the manipulation of the behavioural equations and data, by mathematical and statistical techniques, that imply that the value of some variable or set of variables is being maximised subject to specified constraints.

There are a number of reasons why maximisation plays such a dominant role in economics — not all of which we will go into. In addition to the normal traditions within which economists work, and the nature of their training, part of the emphasis on maximisation models may result from the fact that we possess an exceptionally rich body of mathematical knowledge applicable to problems of maximisation and optimisation. Thus, even economists who are sceptical about various aspects of contemporary microtheory, frequently find it useful to carry out the empirical work they engage in, so that, at the very least implicitly, the notion of maximisation under constraint is assumed.

The basic tradition in microtheory is to assume that households maximise utility, and firms maximise profits. The gradual refinement of economic analysis into more elaborate and more carefully worked out mathematical models, including the work on general equilibrium models, has resulted in establishing this mode of thought through the development of mathematically rigorous conceptualisations of microeconomic theory. In this way the mathematical skill and ingenuity involved in this type of work, especially at its most advanced levels, has helped to increase the acceptability of maximising models. Thus, for a great many economists, economics appears to be primarily the study of maximisation under constraint when applied to various forms of economic behaviour. Some of the alternatives to the profit maximising theory of the firm that have been developed in the last two decades still employ a maximising approach. The main difference is that it is no longer profits that are maximised − other considerations enter. Thus, in Baumol's model,[3] sales revenue is maximised subject to a profit constraint. In Williamson's model,[4] management's utility is maximised and a number of considerations enter the utility function as arguments.

An interesting example of the above, has been the fate of the work of Herbert Simon[5] and his colleagues at Carnegie-Mellon University to introduce into economics modes of thought that do not imply maximisation. The concern here is not with the basic idea of 'satisficing' − which Simon proposed as the most useful approach to non-maximisation thinking in economics − but rather that the work failed in its attempt to have an impact on the work of professional economists. It is noteworthy that the failure of the work of the Carnegie school to win wide acceptance depended not on whether predictions based on these ideas turned out to be correct or not, but was most likely a consequence of the fact that they did not fit into the conventional mode of economic thought.

Despite the fact that there is considerable controversy in the literature about the validity of microeconomic theory, there is, nevertheless, considerable reluctance among economists to adopt an alternative non-maximising approach. In recent years the controversy has emanated, in part, from the Cambridge (England) school, which has argued that the double switching possibility results in a theory of competitive equilibrium that does not guarantee the full employment of labour, and creates some doubts about the meaning of capital valuations.[6] Yet this controversy has not led to the development of an alternative model, nor the acceptance of non-maximising approaches. Despite such considerations, it seems to me that for a number of purposes it might be useful to try a non-maximising approach. This view depends on two basic considerations: (i) a considerable amount of empirical evidence suggests that instances of non-maximising behaviour are frequently observed in practice; (ii) we shall see here, and in later chapters, that a non-maximising approach turns out to be especially useful for the analysis of such problems as the microeconomic influences on the development of inflation.

A resumé of some of the studies which suggest non-maximisation behaviour has been presented by the author elsewhere.[7] In these summary remarks we can do little more than indicate the very general nature of the evidence. Part of this evidence has to do with a variety of instances in which opportunities to increase profits, or decrease losses, are ignored. In some extreme cases, firms returned to inferior practices after more profitable practices had been introduced by consultants who served as advisors to the management in question. Thus, even experience with superior practices is not always sufficient to retain them. An additional type of evidence which may be especially persuasive to some, involves econometric tests of the implications of the theory to be suggested, whose results have turned out to be in accordance with the predictions of the theory. Finally, what is persuasive to some is that those employed by business firms frequently argue that their own experience leads them to believe that maximising behaviour does not in fact take place. For the reasons just stated, as well as others, it seems worthwhile to experiment with models of economic behaviour that do not assume maximising or optimising decision making.

In the chapters that follow we will try to show that in explaining the generation of inflationary pressure in the system, a non-maximising model has certain advantages. This is true for both the supply and demand sides of the process. In developing the analysis we shall deal first with the supply side — that is, with the theory of the firm and the industry, and how the firm and the industry contribute to inflation. We will argue that it is useful to consider firms that neither minimise costs nor maximise profits. This will lead to the analysis of changes in X-efficiency — which in essence involves changes in productivity. We will then examine the impact of productivity changes on inflationary pressure in a world of incomplete and imperfect contracts. Once we assume that firms do not set prices to maximise profits, it becomes easier to take into account emulative behaviour and tacit collusion. Furthermore, we shall argue that relative bargaining power can play a greater role in a non-maximising system than a maximising one. One of the implicit assumptions of much of conventional microtheory is equal bargaining power, but the facts of the world suggest that unequal bargaining power may be a more realistic assumption. Towards the end of this study we will show the relation of these considerations to a non-maximising theory of the household.

A word to readers who are economists may be in order at this juncture. There is frequently a tendency on the part of some economists to try to 'translate' non-maximising models into maximising counterparts. While this can sometimes be done, it loses in directness of exposition and consideration of alternative models of behaviour. That is, in considering alternative models, distinctiveness may be lost if we try to force everything into a maximising framework.

II.   X-Efficiency Theory and Cost Minimisation

A word on the meaning of X-inefficiency. In its simplest sense, X-inefficiency is contrasted to allocative inefficiency. Inputs, or factors of production, may be allocated to the right units for use. However, there is no need to presume that the decision and performance units involved must use inputs as effectively as possible. We refer to the difference between maximal effectiveness of the utilisation of inputs and the actual effectiveness as the degree of X-inefficiency. For present purposes it is of little importance whether we define this in terms of an absolute amount, or as the ratio for which the deviation from maximal effectiveness is the numerator and the amount is the denominator.

Thus, by X-inefficiency, we have in mind all elements having to do with efficiency that are not involved in allocative efficiency. A diagrammatical illustration indicates the nature of its meaning. In Figure 3.1 we consider combinations of capital and labour which produce quantities of output. Q_{min} represents the isoquant that will produce the quantity Q_1 for various combinations of capital and labour. (In each case the minimum amount is used in order to produce the output.) K_a, L_a is the larger amount of capital and labour *actually* required in order to produce the amount Q_1. The difference between the two along a ray from the origin represents the X-efficiency component. In this case it is measured by the difference between the actual quantities of capital and labour as against those that would be used if costs were minimised. Of course X-efficiency can also be measured in terms of actual quantity produced for a given combination

Figure 3.1

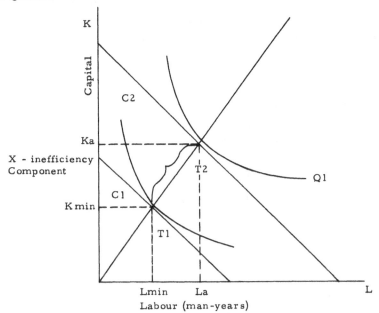

of capital and labour. The concept reflects the idea that it is one thing to allocate inputs to economic units such as firms, but it is something else to use these inputs efficiently. Hence, X-efficiency measures the degree of ineffectiveness in the utilisation of the inputs.

However, X-efficiency is not the same as what is frequently referred to as technical efficiency, since X-efficiency may arise for reasons outside the knowledge or the capability of managers attempting to do the managing. It may arise for reasons entirely outside the firm, or for reasons having to do with choices made by employees who are not themselves managers. In other words, it is not only a matter of technique of management, or anything else 'technical' in carrying out decisions, that is involved in X-efficiency. By X-*in*efficiency we have in mind *decisions* and processes of implementation, that are nonoptimal, and which are an inherent part of organisational life. The basic point of the theory that has been developed around the concept of X-efficiency, is that firms do not minimise costs and, indirectly, do not maximise profits.

We now review very briefly some reasons why X-inefficiency should exist. To start with, we consider firms that have long-run but indefinite contractual arrangements with their members. The nature of such contracts are inevitably incomplete. In other words, contracts do not, and probably in most cases cannot, specify precisely what a firm member is expected to do. All job descriptions are at some points rather vague and require interpretation. In other words, a distinction must be made between the hiring of labour time and the determination of labour output. The contract may specify the labour time aspect — that is, the hours of work that are expected to be kept. However the actual activities that an employee carries out, will depend to some degree on his own choices and those of others with whom he works. The fact that these choices are highly constrained does not deny the related aspect that some degree of choice or discretion is involved. The intervening element between labour time and actual output is basically a nonpurchasable input that we refer to as motivation. Thus all jobs are presumed to require interpretation. These interpretations imply that the person in some sense chooses the activities that he carries out, the pace at which he will carry them out, the quality at which they are carried out, and the time sequence of activities.

There are two aspects to the concept of a job interpretation. One involves the 'effort points' possible in the situation, while the other involves the 'effort positions' chosen out of the set of effort points. By an effort point, we have in mind a bundle of activities and associated characteristics that represents the content of a given *level* of effort. We may specify the content involved in work as the carrying out of a set of activities in a given sequence. But we choose not only between activities (A), but also between alternative pace (P) levels and quality (Q) levels at which each activity is carried out, and the time (T) at which each activity is carried out. Thus an effort point may be viewed as an APQT bundle; that is, a given set of activities, and a specific pace level, quality level and time associated with each activity. Now an *effort position* is a set of effort points. The reason more than one effort point may be required is that the individual inter- preting his or her job, may want to respond differently to different demands made on his or her time. The extent of his or her choice responses inevitably depends on the degree of motivation involved in the context in which work takes place, as well as the capabilities of the individual.

What has all this to do with the question of X-efficiency? Once we introduce the notion of the job interpretation we imply that, at least to some extent, individuals are free to choose the effort levels at which they work. In its turn the effort level determines the value of output that the individual contributes to the firm. Since an individual can choose a variety of effort levels, the productivity of the individual becomes a variable in this system of thought. If we separate the hiring and payment to labour from its productivity, then productivity becomes not only the amount of labour that is higher, but also the nature of the job interpretation made by firm members. Now suppose that this holds for all mem- bers of the firm; it therefore follows that there is no necessity why labour productivity should turn out to be such that output is maximised for a given set of inputs. This in turn implies that costs are not necessarily minimised. Clearly if costs are not minimised, then some degree of X-inefficiency may be said to exist. It is to be noted that this argument follows even if it is true for some members and not all of them.*

* It is of interest that most industries do not use piece rates at all, or use them only partially. There are a variety of technical reasons why this is the case, which we cannot go into here. But, even in the case of piece rates, the individual can still choose a nonoptimal effort position

There are two types of work situation in which motivation is likely to be specially important. The first is work within interdependent teams. That is jobs in which individual effort is part of the team effort and individual productivity is meaningless apart from the team effort. For instance, if it takes four individuals to move a grand piano, one cannot attach meaning to any specific individual in doing the moving job apart from the other three. Clearly, this is a team activity and the effort of any individual, as well as all of them, will depend in part on the motivation of specific individuals, as well as the motivation generated by the social interactions of individuals in the team activity.

Motivation may be viewed as an input, but it is important to bear in mind that it is not an input that is purchased in the market. Rather, it is a consequence of the interactions between individuals within the firm, and the system of payments, promotions and sanctions which the formal management attempts to impose. However, the formally determined motivational system is only a part of the actual motivational system, and, furthermore, the formal system very frequently may not operate the way the management anticipates.

Consider especially the influence of peers on each other. The utility that an individual associates with alternative job interpretations will depend on peer group interactions. Do peers approve or disapprove of the interpretations in question. Similar approval and disapproval mechanisms, and the various ways in which they manifest themselves, will operate with respect to vertical relations – that is those relations determined by the hierarchical structure of the organisation. Thus, the nature of the motivational system will influence job interpretations, and hence determine what individuals do within the work context. As a result, the motivational system helps to determine output. Furthermore, within this system

from the point of view of maximising output for given inputs. Since such nonoptimal choices involve larger indirect costs than would otherwise be the case, this in its turn also implies some degree of X-inefficiency.

of analysis, the formal management does not completely control the motivational system. Individuals who are part of management also have to interpret their jobs. Hence, since management cannot completely control motivation, it cannot determine outputs from given inputs.

A second type of job in which X-inefficiency may be involved is nondirect productivity jobs. This may involve all the staff functions of the firm, or all the activities that do not directly affect the product in some way. Thus elements such as design of the product, accounting and financial details, and various other aspects of the overhead bureaucracy of the firm, may not be directly involved in the product although they certainly involve costs. There is no way of measuring the productivity of individuals engaged in these areas in terms of contributions to product output. But since costs are involved, the motivations that determine the various effort levels also influence costs and will influence the efficiency of the firms.

Whether or not the nature of the production process allows us to measure the individual contributions to output is not a significant issue. As long as there are interpersonal motivational elements involved, there is an aspect of joint determination of output. All of this is not to deny that there may be some instances in which the interpersonal aspects of motivation are unimportant, and in which individuals determine output independently of others. But as long as there are some interdependent motivational influences for some parts of the firm, then the X-efficiency analysis will hold. This seems likely to be a factor in most situations outside of self-sufficient agriculture, or other contexts in which individuals are essentially self-employed, and whose output is separable from the output of other individuals. As long as this is not the case, questions of degrees of X-efficiency are likely to be important.

III.   Theory of Inert Areas

In attempting to explain why X-efficiency should persist, the theory of inert areas, a concept closely related to inertia, is found to be useful.

The theory of inert areas is a very general concept. It can include maximisation as a very special case, but generally this is not the case. To begin with, consider a set of effort positions. An individual in interpreting his job will choose one effort position out of the set. We associate a utility level to each effort *point*. At the same time, we also associate a utility level with each effort *position*, in such a way that it is no higher than the highest utility of an effort point contained in the effort position, and no lower than the lowest utility effort point in the position. In general we presume that the utility associated with an effort position is somewhere in between the effort points that make up the effort position.

Once we have a set of effort positions and its associated utilities, we can specify what we mean by an inert area for effort positions. By an inert area, we have in mind a subset of effort positions such that if a person chooses any one of these positions he has no inclination to move to any other position, despite the fact that there are different utility levels associated with different positions. The reason for this is that we assume in the general case, that there is a utility cost greater than zero in moving from one position to another. Thus the set of utility positions in an inert area will include those positions for which the utility cost of moving from one position to another is always less than the utility gain involved. Among the specific utility costs we have in mind here, are the setting-up cost of establishing oneself in a position, the uncertainty cost involved in a move, the cost involved in shifting away from established routinised procedures, and the costs involved in shifting out of peer and/or supervisory relationships.

We consider briefly each of these costs in turn. An individual does not know at the outset how a job will work out. Thus, there is a normal setting-up cost in establishing oneself within a given job interpretation. There is, in addition, an area of uncertainty surrounding any move from a known position to an unknown one. Within any given job interpretation it is likely an individual will have established certain routine procedures with which the person feels comfortable, and a move involves the cost of re-establishing such procedures in a new effort position. In a great many employment contexts, it is quite likely that the most important utility cost aspect involved is that connected with establishing approved relationships among peers, as well as with those at higher and lower levels in the hierarchy.

Consider the case of peer group influences. To a greater or less degree, most individuals are likely to care about the extent to which others with whom they are in contact on the job approve or disapprove of the way they are handling the job. This is especially likely to be the case if such relationships are instrumental in the work involved, in the sense that the work person A carries out becomes an input into the work individual B tries to carry out. Any shift in effort position is likely to influence some other individuals, and to some degree, is likely to involve reactions of approval or disapproval. Thus the 'disturbance of others' effects of a shift will become part of the utility cost of undertaking such a change. This is also part of the general idea that co-operative productive activities require predictable behaviour on the part of individuals with respect to the behaviour of others, and hence it requires fairly stable expectations as to the performance of others. As a result, there exists the possibility of a considerable utility cost involved in shifting from one effort position to another.

A way of looking at the matter is that, initially, someone in a new job will experiment with a variety of effort positions. At some point he will hit on something that seems to work reasonably well. At this point experimentation stops. In other words, further experimentation no longer yields a utility gain greater than the utility cost of experimentation. In this case the individual may be said to be in an inert area.

This is illustrated in Figure 3.2 in which U represents the utility from effort, and the area from c_1 to c_2 represents the utility cost of moving from one effort position to another. Within the cost bounds there is no incentive to move, and this may be looked upon as an inert area. Hence if, in the process of experimentation, the individual lands in the inert area experimentation stops, even though utility is not maximised.

Figure 3.2

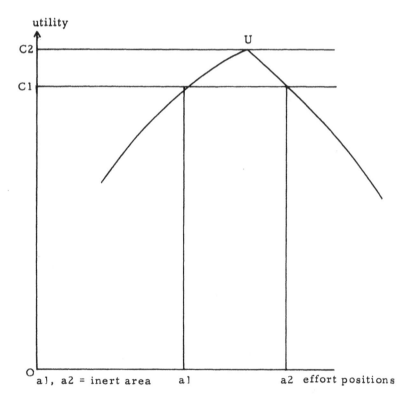

Now consider briefly the case of two individuals in which one supervises the other. Each of them carries out these experiments and each may land in his inert area. The point involved is that, even though the supervisor works fairly efficiently, if the supervisor lands on his inert area, there is no reason for him to maximise X-efficiency in the process of experimentation. If this can be true for any specific supervisor, then such relations can exist throughout the firm, since inert areas are presumed to exist for all members of the firm. Hence there is no reason to presume that in this case costs are minimised, or what is the same thing, that every individual will maximise his effort from the viewpoint of presumed firm objectives.[8] In addition, the individual will resist having effort maximised from someone else's viewpoint, since this would diminish his utility from his job interpretation.

IV. Equilibrium of the Firm and Effort Entropy

If every individual in the firm is in his inert area, then we might view this as an equilibrium state for the firm. No individual is interested in shifting his effort position, unless the events external to the firm alter the utility gain sufficiently so as to stimulate movements by some individuals from existing effort positions to others. It is to be noted that a monopolistic firm, in equilibrium, need not necessarily minimise costs. In the general case we would not expect anything approximating cost minimisation to take place.

Now consider the case of a competitive industry. Each firm produces a product fairly similar to that sold by other firms, and as a result this puts pressure on all firms to sell their product at approximately the same price. However, even in this case we need not presume that cost minimisation takes place. To see this, we introduce the concept of effort entropy. The basic idea is that the effort levels of individuals gradually become less, or less effective, from the viewpoint of the interests of a firm if controls and incentives from top management declines. In other words, one of the main jobs of management is to continually make sure that the monitoring and incentive system maintains a given effort level. This follows from the assumption that all individuals in the firm have a desire to deviate from the constraints of operating in accordance with the firm's goals, at least to some degree.

We should expect that even those at the highest levels in a firm hierarchy need not behave in such a way as to attempt to minimise effort entropy. In other words, the effort positions-utility relation already takes into account the constraints imposed by others in the firm with whom the individual interacts. As these constraints are weakened, some individuals will be induced to change their activities to be more closely in accordance with their own utilities rather than interdependent determined utilities. Recall that an effort position contains a number of effort points not all of which have the same utility to him. The weakening of constraints may result in a shift toward some effort points with higher utility to the individual, but of lower value to the output of the firm. In addition, for some individuals, the weakening of constraint influences on individual behaviour may alter the gains from a shift in effort position so that some are induced to shift to positions of lesser value to the firm.

Thus for a given number of firms, that effort entropy may be sufficiently high so that actual costs are considerably above minimum costs. In addition, there is no reason why entrepreneurship should be in such ample supply that new firms could enter and organise themselves at a more efficient level than the average of the existing firms. Once we assume that there is less than an infinite supply of entrepreneurs, it follows that, given the entropy assumption, there is no reason for an industry which approximates a competitive industry to a result in an equilibrium under which firms minimise their costs of production.

V. Price Setting

How will competition affect the degree of X-efficiency? The level of cost comfortable for the internal organisational structure is not the level that external pressures will permit the firm to maintain. Assume an industry with relatively high costs and a sequence of entering firms at constant intervals. As firms enter, output increases, inventories accumulate, and there is pressure for prices to fall. Lower prices put pressures on existing firms. Firms whose costs are above the new price face eventual extinction or a strong pressure to become more efficient. Members of such firms with inefficient effort positions receive signals and generate pressures for a shift in their effort position, and in the effort positions of others. If the inert areas are not very large etc., then effort increases and costs fall. Where there are very large inert areas, the firm may not survive. To some degree it is replaced by new firms with lower costs. Thus, starting with high degrees of X-inefficiencies, competition creates pressures to reduce X-inefficiency.

How are prices set in the process described in the previous paragraph? Under the theory of inert areas the process of price setting is much looser, and much more a matter of special cases, than in the conventional theory. In accordance with our theory, setting prices is part of the job interpretation of one or more individuals in the firm. In equilibrium the price setting process is fairly constant. That is, we visualise that there exists a pricing formula which is within the inert area of an individual or group within the firm. As long as everything goes well the same pricing formula is used. But in the event of pressures from competition or adversity, the formula is either flexible enough to respond to these pressures, or it is one of the elements subject to change. Consider the most common type of formula, a cost-plus conventional mark-up calculation. The consequence of competition or adversity is increased inventories, or decreased sales, or a reduction in the growth of sales. One possibility of relieving pressures created by increased competition is to reconsider the formula, or adjust some component of it, in order to meet the pressures that have been created. However we must keep in mind that there exist alternatives, of which one is to allow sales to fall (or not grow) and to reduce the planned scale of operations, while at the same time maintaining the usual price formula. Hence we keep in mind that the response to pressure may be a reduction in prices, or it may be a reduction in scale, or some mixture of the two. In cases in which growth is taking place and prices are increasing, the rates of change may fall as a consequence of pressure, but the absolute level of prices in operation may be constant or rise. At the same time we should expect that adversity will put pressure on reducing X-inefficiency, as explained in the previous section. It is important to note that under monopoly these pressures are likely to be much weaker or entirely inoperative.

The point to observe in this theory is that there is no presumption that the price formula used is one that maximises profits.

Another consideration to keep in mind is that the concept of inert area is also applicable to households. Thus the demand side can no longer be portrayed by a demand curve as a thin line, but rather it would have to be pictured as a band that allows for the inert areas involved in the household consumption decisions. The practical significance of this approach is that for very small price changes there may be no change in the quantity purchased. These ideas will be amplified in later sections when we consider specific applications to the problems of inflation and employment.

Notes

1. The ideas summarised in this chapter are expounded in detail in my book, *Beyond Economic Man* (Harvard University Press, Cambridge, Massachusetts, January 1976). The more compressed and more technical version of these ideas is also to be found in Harvey Leibenstein, 'Aspects of the X-Efficiency Theorem of the Firm', *Bell Journal of Economics* (October 1975).

2. See T.W. Schultz (ed.), *Economics of the Family* (University of Chicago Press, 1974).

3. See William J. Baumol, *Business Behavior, Value, and Growth* (The Macmillan Company, New York, 1959).

4. See O.E. Williamson, *The Economics of Discretionary Behavior: Managerial Objectives in a Theory of the Firm* (Markham Publishing Company, Chicago, 1967).

5. See H.A. Simon, 'New Developments in the Theory of the Firm', *American Economic Review*, vol. LII, no. 2 (May 1962), pp. 1-15.

6. For a survey of this controversy see Mark Blaug, *The Cambridge Revolution* (The Institute of Economic Affairs, London, 1974).

7. See H. Leibenstein, 'Allocative Efficiency versus X-Efficiency', *American Economic Review*, vol. 56 (June 1966), pp. 397-409. See also H. Leibenstein, *Beyond Economic Man*, pp. 42-4, for a summary of recent empirical evidence – i.e. the last decade.

8. Incidentally, we can see that maximising behaviour can fit as a special case of inert area. Where the inert area contains only positions of maximum utility, then the situation is trivial. This would be the case where the utility costs of moving are zero. Of course, in this case it does not necessarily follow that if individuals maximise their own utility from the job, that this implies maximising output for the firm. The latter will only be true if the firm in some sense can be said to be able to influence the motivational system, or individual effort levels, in such a way that there is always a coincidence between the interests of the firm, and the interests of individuals employed by the firm.

4 THE IMPORTANCE OF X-EFFICIENCY THEORY FOR INFLATION

I. Microtheory and Inflation

Conventional microtheory has a highly constraining effect on our ability to examine the causes and consequences of inflation on a microeconomic basis. From this viewpoint, X-efficiency theory has a liberating effect. It opens up possibilities for analysis that are closed via the conventional means of thought.

Consider the case in which a general equilibrium is presumed to exist. All markets are in competitive equilibrium, and the system has produced an equilibrium set of *relative* prices. Further suppose that the analytical approach is that of comparative statics. Can anything be said about inflation that is meaningful and sensible under such a scheme of analysis? We will show that very little can be said about inflation, except that it quite naturally leads to what has become known as the monetarist position. The system yields relative prices but not absolute prices.

Our first problem is to decide how absolute prices are to be determined. Instead of assuming that some commodity serves as the *numeraire* (unit of account), let us introduce fiat money immediately with an externally prescribed unit of account. Relative prices are in terms of this unit of account. We assume further that there exists a transactions demand for money and, given this demand, absolute prices are determined by the artificial supply of money, determined by the central monetary authorities. Now, can anything be said about inflation if we stay strictly within the sort of changes usually considered under microtheory? Of course, if some input becomes more scarce and its supply curve moves to the left, this will affect all costs into which the input enters, and as a consequence some prices will rise. Relative to the prices that have risen, other prices will of necessity have to fall. If the overall money supply remains constant, the average price level will not change. Thus, the theory has much to say about changes in relative prices, but from the point of view considered, nothing can be said about the overall price level. In a similar vein one can carry out mental experiments with changes in inputs, outputs, or production functions (and thus include innovations), and still not obtain any change in the general price level. We continue to assume throughout, that the transaction *volume* remains the same, that the transaction demand for money remains the same, and that the supply of money remains the same. Here we must bear in mind that there is no explicit connection between microtheory and the last three variables we have mentioned. They are usually assumed to be external to the theory.

Within the assumptions we have discussed, overall growth will change the general price level. Suppose that each year innovations are introduced so that in each industry ten per cent more output is produced with the same inputs. Suppose also that the *volume* of transactions in the relevant sense remains the same, but each transaction is ten per cent larger. The supply of money remains constant. The necessary equilibrium result would be for *all absolute* prices to fall by ten per cent each year. This represents an overall change in the price level each year, but surely this should not be called deflation. Rather it should be seen as a consequence of growth. A similar argument could be made with respect to declines in productivity as a result of say, the gradual exhaustion of a natural resource that enters all goods. This time we have a general price increase, but it is not the usual type of inflationary phenomenon that concerns us.

Of course if the money supply is increased at a greater rate we can have inflation; but we are now outside microtheory. Money supply changes are usually viewed as exogenous *macro*theory effects and are not part of the microtheory apparatus.

Let us now leave the growth area. An artificial possibility worth considering is one which involves a change in the unit of account. Suppose all old dollars are now arbitrarily called *two* dollars, and all old currency is changed for new currency in the new unit of account. What consequences follow from a microtheoretical viewpoint? In terms of old dollars, we have a change in the absolute price level. Suppose further that the event we have just described occurs every year. In terms of original dollars, we will have a 100 per cent rate of inflation every year. But is this *true* inflation? Is this the type of inflation that is likely to concern anybody?

Let us examine the consequences of this type of 'inflation'. With one *possible* exception, the consequences are zero. The possible exception involves the case in which some contracts for future payments are interpreted in current dollars, rather than the current value of the dollars at the time the contract is made. To further our analysis, assume that no such contracts (or such interpretations of contracts) exist. In that case, although formally 100 per cent inflation per year exists, there are no consequences. Essentially all that has happened is that every year the name of the unit of account has changed. Nobody's real income is any different than it would be if the unit of account had not changed, nor are the *real* values of any assets different they they would be otherwise. All relative prices remain the same throughout. Whether or not we call the phenomenon we have just described by the name 'inflation' is of no importance. The point is, it is the sort of phenomenon that no one would care anything about. In fact, this artificial example suggests, precisely by what it leaves out, what it is we care about when we are concerned about the phenomenon of inflation.

What matters to people is that inflation *normally* (not the artificial type we have just described) does change relative prices, does change the relative values of stocks compared to flows, and, above all, it does change relative incomes and the distribution of income in a seemingly arbitrary fashion. It is precisely for these reasons that a theory of *relative* prices, in which money as such does not enter as an argument, is quite useless, if not misleading, in trying to help us understand the phenomenon of inflation.

The basic point of this study is that the conventional microtheory which is so strongly embedded in the minds of many economists, is an element that interferes with the proper analysis of inflation, and that the X-efficiency theory liberates us from much of this mode of thought. We will show that the X-efficiency approach allows for the introduction of differential bargaining power, whereas the current micro approach makes it difficult to do so. However, before going further, let us consider briefly some variants of the current approach.

II. Expectations

Let us keep in mind that the essence of the inflation we care about lies in the fact that, at least temporarily, it causes redistributions of income and wealth. A popular approach to the inflation problem is to introduce expectations. We consider as before a competitive economy with strong forces or regulations that maintain competition in each industry, and hence there will exist a strong tendency towards competitive equilibrium. Now suppose that everyone expects that next year there will be a 10 per cent increase in *all* prices. Never mind, for the time being, where such expectations come from. Suppose contracts are made annually. Every buyer and seller will now take such expectations into account. Tastes and marginal productivities are the same as before. Such expectations will be self-fulfilling. Everyone will make contracts at prices that are 10 per cent higher than before. Thus, those whose income depends on the value of their marginal productivities are no worse off than before. Buyers of inputs pay 10 per cent more for all inputs, and their sales prices are proportionally higher.

What about the relation between stocks and flows? Each year inventories are worth 10 per cent more than the year before. At first blush it might appear that for those who invest in inventories there will be an inflationary profit of 10 per cent. But this would not occur under perfect markets with 'neutral' money. The interest rate plus storage costs, the opportunity costs of carrying inventories, would also rise by 10 per cent, and the effect of expectations on the price of goods held as inventories should lead to an outcome where no one is any better off than before. Two elements emerge from this example. The mere introduction of expectations into a system of perfect markets, including perfect future markets, that determine relative prices, does not change the outcome. The outcome can be changed by a non-neutral monetary policy, and hence it suggests that the type of mind set that works in terms of neoclassical perfect markets as an approximation to reality, is also likely to be attracted to a monetarist position if the person involved cares about consistency.

Thus far in discussing inflation we have assumed away one major difficulty: in what prices are contracts made? Are they made in current (monetary) prices or in real prices? Suppose that everyone has the same expectation of inflation and that contracts are made in current prices. One can work out an argument on this basis, and the usual full employment assumptions that result in redistribution of income. The argument runs somewhat as follows. Since prices are expected to rise, the present values of inventories and capital goods are worth more than would otherwise be the case. In other words, the present value of the stream of quasi-rents attributable to capital goods will rise. This stimulates a higher investment in capital than otherwise. We assume as usual diminishing returns to capital. The capital/labour ratio is higher than otherwise. Thus, the rate of return per unit of capital is lower, and the return to labour relatively higher than otherwise.

What happens to income shares is difficult to determine

in this situation. It is not possible to determine on *a priori* grounds whether or not the lower return to capital is, or is not, counter-balanced by the greater amount of capital in this case than in the case without inflation. The answer is indeterminate. What is more important is that even if it were determinate it would not be especially useful. The assumptions on which this mode of analysis is based are too constricting. These are: (i) full employment of labour, (ii) the existence of equilibrium in all markets, (iii) labour is homogenous, and (iv) in some sense equal bargaining power of all parties is implicitly assumed.

The essence of the argument presented above is to equate inflation at a given interest rate to what is essentially a lower *real* interest rate. Thus, if the monetary authorities expand the money supply at some given interest rate so that prices rise, then the real cost of funds is lower, since the real interest rate is equal to the nominal interest rate plus the rate of price increase. Hence the argument is really reduced to the effects of a reduction in the real interest rate. We should keep in mind that, in equilibrium, the interest rate is equal to the profit rate where the profit is discounted for risk. Hence a reduction of the interest rate results in an increase in investment, until the profit rate falls into line with the interest rate. The outcome depends on whether investment is elastic, or relatively inelastic, with respect to the interest rate. If investment is inelastic, the share going to capital falls and we will have a redistribution of income in favour of labour. If the investment is relatively elastic with respect to the interest rate, then the opposite outcome will occur.[1]

Of course, effects on relative prices can occur, if those in the market have different expectations for future prices of some commodities as against others. But we do not really have a theory of differential expectations for different commodities. Furthermore, if these expectations reflect actual differential scarcities that will occur in the future, then inflation in the usual sense is not involved. If the expectations turn out to be erroneous, then we should expect such erroneous contracts to be temporary, and we should not expect them to be all in one direction. Finally, we should expect them to be corrected in the next period. There seems little analytical promise that we can expect from this approach as long as we keep the assumption of approximately perfect markets.[2]

III.   Monopoly

Let us drop the perfect competitive market assumption. Suppose that part of the economy is composed of a number of industries, each of which is operated as a single firm monopoly. Does that change the situation? Monopolies can behave as they wish and charge any price they wish. They are not constrained by the prices and outputs of other firms. But microtheory claims that monopolies operate in a specific determinate way − they set prices so as to maximise profits. While monopoly prices are different from competitive prices, they are determinate. There is nothing that monopolies do to cause sustained inflation as long as the ratio of goods sold by them remains the same. If the degree of monopoly in the economy increases, then monopoly prices on the average will rise compared to competitive prices, but there is no reason for *all* prices on the average to rise so long as we keep our analysis within the bounds of conventional microtheory.[3] Thus even introducing monopolies into the picture does not really help to explain inflation as long as we assume that they behave in the conventional manner − that is, and this is most important, as long as we assume that monopolies *minimise* costs and set prices so as to maximise profits.

Oligopoly is more difficult to discuss in this connection. The basic problem arises from the fact that oligopoly theory is not well developed. No widely-accepted theory exists. But to the extent that bits of theory do exist, these bits are not connected with monetary phenomenon. Hence in this area also, from a strictly theoretical viewpoint, nothing has really been established between oligopoly behaviour and inflation – and, in particular, nothing can be said about the process of sustained inflation. Oligopolists are by definition very sensitive to the behaviour of other firms. An argument has been made that oligopoly prices tend to be sticky (cf. Sweezy's kinked demand curve theory), but there is no reason why there should *always* be an upward bias under oligopoly conditions. In fact, we should expect that price stickiness should be a general price stabilising force rather than an inflationary force. Furthermore, in a mixed economy in which there is both competitive and oligopoly sectors, there is reason for oligopoly to distort *relative* prices as a consequence of price stickiness in the oligopoly sector, but there is nothing in the theory to suggest that the overall absolute price level must rise. Once again *absolute* price determining factors or influences are not easily introduced if we stay within the intellectual mould and constraints of conventional price theory.

One may look at all these arguments from a more general and abstract viewpoint. First, we must keep in mind the basic argument that the aspect of inflation that is of interest lies in the fact that real inflations do affect, and sometimes seriously so, both income distributions and wealth distributions. However, a nonmonetary theory that determines all relative prices, irrespective of the type of the theory (e.g. conventional theory or Prero Straffa's Ricardian type theory), will also determine income and wealth distributions, and hence will prove to be incapable of handling the inflation process in an essential way. This is obvious once we consider that neither the Fisher or Cambridge equations of money contain relative prices as elements of their theories.

IV. X-Efficiency Theory

Now let us look at X-efficiency theory from the viewpoint of the considerations treated in this section. The previous description of X-efficiency theory should have indicated that it does not assume the behavioural constraints of conventional theory. For present purposes three elements of the theory have to be kept in mind: (i) the concept of inert areas, (ii) the deduction that firms do not minimise costs, and (iii) the notion that the firms use 'conventional' but temporary price formulas that do not maximise profits. Since prices are not set by profit maximising calculations, there is nothing to prevent a firm from raising absolute prices. Furthermore, and most important, the theory of inert areas tells us that if Firm A raises its price Firm B need not follow suit, even if Firm A's act affects Firm B to some degree — or in any event Firm B need not follow suit immediately. Thus this theory already has the possibility of an increase in absolute prices, and not only relative prices. In addition, the fact that firms do not minimise costs, allows for cost increases (for any reason, including adverse bargains for inputs) to result in absolute price increases without other firms changing their absolute prices. How all of this is related to the money supply we consider in a later chapter. All that we hope to suggest here is the relative flexibility of X-efficiency theory compared to conventional theory, with respect to treating the process of inflation.

The main point is that inflation could be viewed as an external event which affects the real purchasing power of individuals, unless they do something to change the contractual basis which determines the income they receive from their jobs, or from the ownership of assets, including such rights to income as pensions and social security payments. It is obvious that if real income is not to decline as a consequence of inflation *recontracting* has to take place. That is, employees have to recontract in order to receive higher wages in an attempt to maintain real wages, and producers of goods, in the cases where the prices of inputs are higher, have to recontract the prices at which they sell their goods. The conventional theory does not specify how contracts are made, when they are made, nor the procedure for *initiating* contracts or attempts at recontracting. But to understand the effect of inflation we have to understand these procedures, and how they are induced and determined. In other words, we must understand who has the capacity to initiate recontracting, whether such initiatives will be accepted or not by the other parties, and the factors that determine the outcome of attempts to recontract.

The theory of inert areas turns out to be a very convenient vehicle for handling these considerations. The size and nature of the inert area, compared to the impact of the inflation change, will determine to what extent initiatives are taken for recontracting. At the same time a consideration of bargaining power will indicate whether such initiatives are likely to be successful or unsuccessful. More on this in the ensuing chapters.

It is of special interest to note that introducing the theory of inert areas for households creates a situation in which industries with many firms approximate monopolistic competition, whether or not there is significant product differentiation. The reason is that the inert areas for households will allow specific sellers to raise their prices to some degree and not lose all of their customers, as would be the case under perfect competition. In addition, if we have a relatively inelastic supply of entrepreneurs (as seems likely to be the case in many industries in developing countries), then this results in the existence of monopolistic profits. That is, profits greater than competitive equilibrium profits. If we apply marginal productivity theory to this area, then this will turn out to be a case under which the value of marginal products of the various agents of production would not exhaust the net revenue of the firm. As a result, in this case, even if we accept marginal productivity theory as the appropriate way of determining the lower bound of the payments to contributors to output, there is still a surplus over which relative bargaining power can determine the outcome.

Notes

1. Harry Johnson has suggested another possibility why inflation might result in a shift of the income distribution towards labour: 'if inflation leads to a substitution for the use of money of other methods of effecting transactions, and these methods are relatively labour-intensive (e.g. more frequent wage-payments and more frequent trips to the shops) inflation will increase the labour-intensity of overall economic activity and hence tend to redistribute income towards labour (other things being assumed equal, of course, which they probably will not be).' Harry G. Johnson, *The Theory of Income Distribution* (Gray-Mills Publishing Ltd, London, 1973), preface.

2. We ignore in this analysis two types of theories that have evolved considerable interest in connection with the analysis of inflation. The first of these is the Phillips curve type of analysis and the second is information search theory. We can safely ignore the Phillips curve analysis on several grounds. To begin with it is a macro type of theory. In addition it seems clear that it is inapplicable at the present time, even to advanced economies. Finally, it was never really intended to be applicable to developing countries. For a discussion on this type of theory see James Tobin, 'The Wage-Price Mechanism: Overview of the Conference', *The Econometrics of Price Determination*, conference sponsored by Board of Governors of the Federal Reserve System, and Social Science Research Council (Board of Governors of the Federal Reserve System, Washington, DC, June 1972), pp. 5-15.

The information-search cost type of theories developed by E.S. Phelps and others is of considerable importance in helping to explain the simultanous existence of market equilibrium and unemployment on a microeconomic basis. However, it does not seem to be helpful in explaining the process of sustained inflation. See E.S. Phelps *et al.*, *Microeconomic Foundations of Employment and Inflation Theory* (Norton, New York, 1970), and especially the perspective paper by William D. Nordhaus, 'Recent Developments in Price Dynamics', *The Econometrics of Price Determination*, conference sponsored by Board of Governors of the Federal Reserve System, and Social Science Research Council (Board of Governors of the Federal Reserve System, Washington, DC, June 1972), pp. 20-31.

3. All prices would rise in the special case in which monopolies produce inputs for *all* non-monopolistic industries.

5 THE IMPACT OF INFLATION ON DEVELOPING COUNTRIES

Despite the fact that there is worldwide concern with the problem of inflation, there is very little work on the consequences of inflation for developing countries, especially on the extent that the distribution of income is affected. We have stressed that the significance of inflation lies in the fact that some gain and some lose through the inflationary process. Nevertheless, there is very little empirical evidence at present to suggest which segments of the population are gainers as against losers. We are forced, therefore, to resort to making logical guesses about the impact of inflation in the absence of hard data and systematic studies. We will return to this problem in the following section.

Two categories of losers are those whose income is derived from assets based on original cash valuations, and those whose bargaining power in the market from which they receive their income is relatively weak. Thus, those who are retired, or unemployed and who receive a portion of their income from money savings or other sources based on cash valuations, are the classically well known losers in the inflationary process. This group is in no way unique to developing countries.

While a good deal of analysis on the impact of inflation holds for both developed and developing countries, our objective is to emphasise the impact on developing countries. Towards this end, it becomes necessary to specify some general characteristics of developing countries and to see if they lead us toward any useful and interesting hypotheses of inflation's impact.

A frequent characteristic of many developing countries is a rapid rate of urbanisation, which is often accompanied by rapid migration from the countryside to towns and cities.

This will normally create a class of temporarily unemployed, as well as a large group of unskilled or semi-skilled workers who have recently joined the urban labour force. In view of the fact that this portion of the workforce is likely to find itself in a position of having to compete for jobs with other workers, their bargaining power is likely to be relatively weak. As a consequence, these groups are likely to lose out during the inflationary process. This is not to argue that their wages never increase as general prices rise, but to imply that compared with other groups such increases are likely to exist with a more persistent lag than the group with more bargaining power.

A subdivision of the group considered above is likely to involve domestic servants in urban areas. The rapid rate of migration creates a supply of potential domestic servants and hence reduces their bargaining power. However, the situation for domestics is ameliorated to a considerable degree (only with respect to inflation) due to the fact that a considerable portion of the domestics' income is likely to be in kind, i.e. housing and food.

Another common characteristic of developing economies is a significant sector composed of self-sufficient farms. To the extent that agricultural incomes are created outside the cash economy, such farmers do have a hedge against inflation.

An interesting group which is difficult to analyse is the civil service. Where the civil service has no political influence of any sort, directly or indirectly, they are likely to be in a poor bargaining position and, as a consequence, lose in the inflationary process. On the other hand, it is frequently the case that the civil service forms an elite group tied (to some extent) to those with strong political influence and, hence, civil service salaries may be indexed. This is not to deny the lags that exist in such cases, but these are likely to be somewhat shorter than for groups without political influence.

An unusually depressed group in developing countries are those who produce commodities subject to price controls.

This is frequently the case for those who produce basic goods such as rice. It would take us too far afield to analyse at this point the relation between price controls, their impact, and the nature of inflation.

Some of the previous remarks clearly suggest that inflation, and the reaction to inflation, is likely to be a politically sensitive area. It is one of the major areas in which economic and political considerations intersect. As a result, part of the analysis of inflation should take into account special governmental help to different groups as a consequence of political considerations. However, it seems unlikely that we could generalise this aspect apart from suggesting that groups that directly or indirectly have political influence will suffer less than groups that do not.

A number of developing countries depend on trade in primary products for which significant substitutes exist, such as coffee, cocoa, rice, etc. These are to be contrasted to such products as oil, for which substitution is much more difficult. In cases of sensitive primary products, it is usually possible for governments to manipulate the price received by farmers versus the price that goods sell for on international markets and, as a result, this is likely to be an area where the political aspects of inflation will be significant.

An unusual aspect of the literature on the impact of inflation on developing countries is that there is *almost no systematic* work available. In particular, systematic work which assessed the gains and losses to various segments of the population as a consequence of inflation should exist, and is certainly feasible, but is absent. A systematic analysis would look upon the inflation process as a zero-sum game which takes real income from some and distributes it to others. Even if this were done on a group-by-group basis, it would only average the gains and losses of the different groups, despite the fact that there are gains and losses within any group. Even this sort of information would be extremely revealing. Yet, from an empirical viewpoint, no studies of this sort exist. Although, once the question is raised (and it seems an obvious one), it suggests some obvious types of exercises and calculations; if not raised, it simply does not seem to come up as an important intellectual issue among development economists. Most of the work concentrates on the *causes* of inflation rather than on the consequences. Perhaps part of our difficulty in understanding causes of inflation is because so little systematic work has been done on the consequences.

There are of course intrinsic difficulties in doing the sort of studies suggested in the previous paragraph. The data are not likely to come in pure form, but are likely to involve changes as a consequence of economic growth and decline, as well as the differential productivity of different sectors. In other words, actual economic operations work normally as positive-sum games in some periods and as negative-sum games in others. In order to express the purely redistributive aspects of inflation, we would have to find a means of separating the non-zero-sum aspects out of the data to arrive at the net zero-sum consequence involved.

These remarks are of some importance as intellectual guidelines to the few studies that touch on aspects of the redistributive consequences of inflation. What these con- siderations suggest is that we have to be particularly wary of partial accounts of gains and losses, since we really cannot determine what actually happened unless we have a complete account. For example, we cannot know how to assess the results of a gambling game in a given period in which ten players played, if all that we know is the winnings or losses of the three players we happened to have questioned. The situation is even more complex if such a game is not zero- sum in that an undetermined cut goes to the casino where the game is played. Nevertheless the few studies that exist are of interest and we will consider some of these below.

A serious attempt to evaluate the impact of inflation on economic development was made by U Tun Wai in 1959.[1] After working with data for 31 countries, Wai came to the conclusion that there was insufficient data, and, to the extent that data does exist, the relationship was inconclusive.

One of the classic studies of inflation, but not of less developed countries (LDCs), is that by Bresciani-Turroni[2] on the hyper-inflation in Germany after World War I. Bresciani-Turroni immediately runs into problems in trying to disentangle the consequences of World War I from the consequences of the inflation of 1918 to 1923. Keeping this difficulty in mind, some interesting conclusions emerge. As a whole, entrepreneurs gained in the inflation while real wages fell. Inflation appears to have destroyed the old middle class as a group of investors and in its place created a new middle class of intermediate traders and small speculators. Further, inflation brought about a general redistribution of income and thereby increased the inequality of income. Favoured industries produced war-related products. This altered the structure of debts, which were repaid in depreciated currency. Thus, creditors lost in favour of debtors. One of the important aspects not considered in detail, is the impact of inflation on wage differentials. Despite real wages decreasing, certain portions of the work force gained, or lost less than others. Those at higher skill levels did more poorly than those with lower skill levels. This brief summary of results hardly does justice to Bresciani-Turroni's work. Nonetheless, it indicates some possible consequences that may result from inflation.

Two of the more determinate studies that suggest fairly clear-cut results with respect to developing countries are by Werner Baer[3] on Brazil and A.P. Gupta[4] on India.

In general, Baer argues that inflation in Brazil 'acted as a mechanism for transferring resources from the consuming to the investing sector, be it governmental or private'.[5] For the time period extending from the late forties to the early sixties, Baer offers the evidence presented in Table 5.1,[6] which demonstrates clearly that the Brazilian government was a larger investor than saver, and, that this was accomplished through the inflationary process.

The argument here is that the weakness of the labour sector, partly as a result of stern control over labour unions

Table 5.1: Savings and Capital Formation of the Private and Government Sectors as a Proportion of Gross Domestic Income

Year	Private Sector		Public Sector		Balance of Payments Deficit on Current Account
	Savings	Capital Formation	Savings	Capital Formation	
1947	12	14	4	3	2
1948	14	14	4	4	0
1949	10	10	4	5	1
1950	12	8	2	5	−1
1951	13	17	5	5	3
1952	16	17	4	6	4
1953	15	11	1	4	0
1954	19	19	4	5	1
1955	17	14	2	5	0
1956	17	13	1	4	0
1957	16	12	1	7	2
1958	12	10	5	9	2
1959	16	14	6	10	2
1960	14	12	5	10	3

Source: computed from national accounts' figures of the Fundacao Getulio Vargas by I. Kerstenetsky.

Table 5.2: Ratio of Wages Paid to Workers to Value Added

Year	All Manufacturing Industries	Textiles	Food Products	Basic Metals Industries and Metal Products	Machinery
1949	23	30	14	27	32
1955	24	32	18	27	32
1956	24	32	16	25	30
1957	23	35	16	25	31
1958	21	32	15	23	28
1959	19	29	14	21	23.5

Sources: computed from IBGE, *Censo Industrial*, 1950 and 1960; and IBGE, *Producao Industrial do Brasil*, 1955, 1956, 1957, 1958.

Table 5.3: Agricultural Prices (1953 = 100)

Year	Cost of Living (Guanabara) Total	Cost of Living (Guanabara) Agric.	Food Prods. (excl. cof.)	Wholesale Prices of Veg. Origin (excl. cof.)	Of Animal Origin	All Food Prods.: Stage of Production[a]
1947	56	52	49	49	35	36
1948	58	55	56	60	43	43
1949	61	58	59	62	45	49
1950	67	63	57	56	51	60
1951	75	71	64	59	68	71
1952	87	85	84	78	90	85
1953	100	100	100	100	100	100
1954	122	121	116	112	122	131
1955	151	151	141	134	155	142
1956	182	187	171	172	170	163
1957	212	215	195	192	191	173
1958	243	246	211	204	216	185
1959	338	357	301	310	271	246
1960	437	466	411	357	508	331
1961	583	627	561	458	755	441
1962	884	1,015	903	777	1,157	726
1963	1,507	1,680	1,512	1,342	1,815	1,153

Note: a. All food products: stage of production — represents prices received by producer.

Source: Conjunctura Economica, June 1963.

Table 5.4: Trends in Lowest and Highest Annual Real Earnings

Year	Earnings in Industries			Earnings in States/Union Territories		
	Lowest Earnings (rupees)	Highest Earnings (rupees)	Col. 2 as % of Col. 3	Lowest Earnings (rupees)	Highest Earnings (rupees)	Col. 5 as % of Col. 6
1	2	3	4	5	6	7
1951	752	1,368	55.0	665	1,293	51.4
1961	834	1,546	53.9	925	1,377	67.2
1962	1,012	2,411	42.0	1,117	1,912	58.4
1970	1,024	2,144	47.8	1,196	1,712	69.9
% change in earnings:						
1951-61	10.9	13.0	—	39.1	6.5	—
1962-70	1.2	−11.1	—	7.1	−10.5	—

Source: based on data in *Indian Labour Statistics*.

by the government in the late fifties,[7] resulted in a decrease in the share of wages in gross domestic income.[8] Essentially, labour did not receive its productivity gains in terms of *real* wages. In evidence of this, Baer offers data on the ratio of wages to value added presented in Table 5.2.[9] Baer's argument is that inflation did not distort resource allocation but contributed to economic growth through the mechanism of forced savings.

One element that also becomes clear in Baer's analysis is the role of the middlemen. Baer argues that unlike the urban sector the agricultural sector did not lose as a consequence of inflation; the net gainers were the various middlemen who were able to skim the difference between the price of food and what was paid to agricultural growers. Table 5.3[10] is clear evidence of this assertion.

Gupta attempts to analyse the effects of inflation on income distribution in India between 1959 and 1972. Part of the argument presented is that higher income groups are able to avoid taxes while somewhat lower income groups, whose incomes are obtained from wages and salaries, are not in a position to do so.[11] Hence, with inflation, and with a lag in the adjustment of marginal tax rates, those who are not self-employed suffer a relative redistributive loss.

Examining the differential impacts between the rural poor and urban poor, Gupta argues that the rural poor spend a higher proportion of their income on food relative to their urban counterparts. As a result they were harder hit by the inflation in food prices in India.[12]

With respect to incomes of factory workers, the analysis by Gupta demonstrates that with inflation there is a narrowing of the gap between the lowest and higher paid workers. Hence, in real terms, higher paid workers appear to suffer a relative redistributive loss as a consequence of inflation.[13] Table 5.4[14] substantiates this point. The situation appears to be more complex with respect to factor shares. Two elements, acting simultaneously, are involved here. On the one hand, real wages fell less than the effective price of

Table 5.5: Trends in Factory Employment, Productive Capital Employed, Ex-factory Value of Output and Value Added by Manufacture, 1959-69

Year	Employment (millions)	Productive Capital (million rupees)	Ex-factory Value of Output (million rupees)	Value Added by Manufacture (million rupees)
1	2	3	4	5
1959	2.87	17,374	26,914	7,950
1960	2.90	19,995	31,504	8,644
1961	3.05	23,742	36,933	9,879
1965	3.99	64,441	64,923	17,004
1966	3.98	76,811	72,478	18,317
1968	3.97	90,061	86,368	20,673
1969	4.15	98,945	99,829	24,959
% compound annual rate of increase:				
1959-69	3.8	19.0	14.0	12.6
1959-65	5.6	24.4	15.8	14.4
1965-9	1.0	11.3	11.4	10.1

Note: The data in columns 3, 4 and 5, being in money terms, cannot be compared as they stand with the data in column 2; but even if they were adjusted for the rise in the price level, the rate of growth of factory employment in recent years would still be found to have been much slower than that of productive capital employed, ex-factory value of output and value added by manufacture.

Source: The data relate to the census sector (all industries) of the Annual Survey of Industries, which now covers all registered factories employing 50 or more workers with the aid of power, or 100 or more workers without the aid of power. The data are collected from the factories each year on a complete enumeration basis and are published in *Annual Survey of Industries*.

Table 5.6: Wage Costs, Taxes and Return on Capital in the Private Corporate Sector, 1965/6 and 1970/1

Distribution of Value Added	1965/6 (million rupees)	1970/1 (million rupees)	% of Total Wage Costs, Taxes and Return on Capital	
			1965/6	1970/1
WAGE COSTS	*6,865.7*	*10,728.1*	*46.0*	*43.9*
Salaries, wages and bonus payments	6,215.0	9,526.9	41.7	39.0
Provident funds	345.6	621.6	2.3	2.5
Employee welfare expenses	305.1	579.6	2.0	2.4
TAXES	*5,363.8*	*9,216.6*	*36.0*	*37.7*
Excise duty and cess	3,697.7	7,065.9	24.8	28.9
Corporation tax	1,666.1	2,150.7	11.2	8.8
RETURN ON CAPITAL	*2,684.5*	*4,513.8*	*18.0*	*18.5*
Interest	1,017.2	1,978.6	6.8	8.1
Profits after tax	1,667.3	2,535.2	11.2	10.4
TOTAL	*14,914.0*	*24,458.5*	*100.0*	*100.0*

Source: 'Finances of Medium and Large Public Limited Companies, 1970-71' in *Reserve Bank* (of India Bulletin, Bombay), September 1972, p. 1430.

capital. Consequently there was a shift to more capital inten-
sive technology.[15] This resulted in a greater reduction in
factory employees than would otherwise have been the
case.[16] Table 5.5[17] confirms this point. As a result, the wage
component in value added by manufacturing decreased.[18]
Table 5.6 verifies this point for India.

In this case one could argue that the redistributive loss
falls mostly on the unemployed, or on those who are forced
to take lower paying jobs than would be the case if they had
been employed in manufacturing. However, no data exist on
what happens to those who would otherwise be employed in
the manufacturing sector. By the very nature of the situation
it would be difficult to obtain such data, even in the best of
circumstances.

In general, we are able to obtain only partial evidence on
the redistributive effects of inflation. At this stage no clear-
cut, systematic and general picture emerges from a review of
the very limited empirical evidence available.

Notes

1. U Tun Wai, 'The Relation between Inflation and Economic
Development: a Statistical Inductive Study', *International Monetary
Fund Staff Papers*, vol. 7 (October 1959), p. 302.

2. Constantino Bresciani-Turroni, *The Economics of Inflation*
(George Allen and Unwin Ltd, London, 1937).

3. Werner Baer, *Industrialization and Economic Development in
Brazil* (Richard D. Irwin, Inc., Homewood, Ill., 1965).

4. A.P. Gupta, 'Inflation, Income Distribution and Industrial Relations in India', *International Labour Review*, vol. 110, no. 2 (August
1974), pp. 165-82.

5. Baer, *Industrialization and Economic Development in Brazil*, p.
110.

6. Ibid., p. 103. Table 5.1 is Baer's Table 5-2 reproduced in total.

7. Ibid., p. 124.

8. Ibid., p. 119.

9. Ibid., p. 120. Table 5.2 is Baer's Table 5-11 reproduced in total.

10. Ibid., p. 153. Table 5.3 is Baer's Table 7-2 reproduced in total.

11. Ibid., p. 171.

12. Ibid., p. 166.

13. Gupta, 'Inflation, Income Distribution and Industrial Relations in India', p. 175.

14. Ibid., p. 175. Table 5.4 is Gupta's Table 3 reproduced in total.

15. Ibid., p. 175.

16. Ibid., p. 176.

17. Ibid., p. 176. Table 5.5 is Gupta's Table 4 reproduced in total.

18. Ibid., p. 176.

19. Ibid., p. 177. Table 5.6 is Gupta's Table 5 reproduced in total.

6 INCOMPLETE CONTRACTS, BARGAINING AND INFLATION

I. Introduction

It is well to keep in mind simultaneously what may be viewed as two possible sides of the inflation experience: (i) the rise in absolute prices for a given output, and (ii) a rise in absolute prices as a consequence of a fall in productivity for the same level of employment. The latter may be more difficult to detect, but it may frequently be an important component of the inflation process. The implicit argument here is that inflation processes are unlikely to be determined by a single aspect or component, but rather inflation should be seen as a process that involves an amalgam of components. Some discussions of inflation given the impression that only one component exists, or that only one component plays a major role. For example, discussions of either demand-pull or 'cost-push' inflations frequently have this flavour.

A word about the nature of the analysis we are working towards is appropriate at this juncture. We have suggested that conventional microtheory has either nothing to say about inflation, or inflation is handled through an arbitrary superimposition onto the microtheory of what is really a macro money supply analysis. The micro process of inflation creation somehow disappears. Above all, in the analysis to be developed in this essay, we want to retain the micro process as part of a significant element in the phenomenon of inflation.

A basic message of microtheory is that a great deal of what happens in an economy is the consequence of many millions of small decisions by millions of decision makers. The argument to be pushed in this essay is that the same thing holds true for the inflation process. Millions of small decisions

65

contribute to that process, but to some degree such decisions are interdependent and *systematic*. Hence it is capable of being understood and analysed. But, before we can do so, we must release ourselves from the analytical prison that conventional microtheory puts us in, in connection with this particular problem area.

To begin with, conventional theory assumes (albeit implicitly) perfect and complete contracts between the firms and its members. For ease of exposition we shall use the terms firm members and employees interchangeably, but by employees we shall have in mind not only what are frequently viewed as employees but also the highest levels of management, including owners who work for the firm where private enterprise firms are involved.

Perfect and complete contracts allow the firm to pay employees in accordance with their productivity, wherever productivity can be calculated. Of course we must keep in mind the usual conventional simultaneous assumptions that the firm makes such contracts in accordance with its presumed objective of minimising costs, while employees aim to maximise their income. Now, suppose we drop these assumptions, what is likely to happen to the various elements of the presumed implicit complete contract?

II.   Incomplete Contracts and Falling Performance

Suppose labour contracts are incomplete, as indeed they invariably are — which elements are specified (or explicitly negotiated) and which are likely to be left out, that is, to be in the incomplete part of the contract. To put the matter in a nutshell, the absolute money payment part is likely to be fairly explicit and well understood by both parties, but the effort-performance element is likely to be incomplete. This is not to suggest that there are never any understandings which are made explicit with respect to performance, but we do suggest that such understandings, by

their very nature, can cover only a part of the effort-performance picture. In most or all cases, there are always non-
insignificant elements of performance that are outside the
explicitly agreed elements of performance. For example,
employees may explicitly agree to be within an area designated as the place of work for 40 hours per week, but the
contract may not specify at all how hard they should work
once they are there. We have argued previously that some
elements of effort (e.g. activities chosen, or pace, or sequence,
or quality of activities) are effectively a variable to employees.
To a greater or lesser degree they can affect some of these
elements. Obviously by affecting some of these elements,
they can affect productivity and output. Thus, the effort
decisions of individuals, which are part of the incomplete
contract of the employment relation contract, can influence
inflation since the money payment part of the contract is
explicit.

To say that some parts of an employment contract are
complete is similar, although not identical, to saying that
some parts of the contract are invariant, and some parts allow
for variations. To allow us to pursue the argument further,
suppose that the money payment to employees is the
invariant part of the contract, and that the employee
performance part is implicit, indeterminate and variable.
Suppose also that the pricing formula used by the firms is a
cost plus a fixed percentage mark-up. Suppose further that
this holds for the entire economy, what then follows? The
money incomes of all firm members are now determined
by their contracts. However, effort and prices of goods are
not determined. To start with, consider three possibilities:
(i) Effort for all employees remains constant. Therefore costs
remain constant and prices remain constant. Nothing of
much interest happens here. (ii) Suppose effort rises and
costs fall and prices fall. This is an important and interesting
case involving economic growth — but we shall leave this to a
later section. (iii) Our main interest here is with the third
possibility — effort falls, costs rise and prices rise accordingly.

This is a clear-cut case of inflation but it's more than that. The total costs of goods available for sale is higher than the contractual payments to all employees. Unless there is an increase of credit available to buyers, or a reduction in the savings of buyers, asset levels remaining the same, some goods must remain unsold. Demand in physical terms will appear to have declined.

Now, we contrast this contract with what may be viewed as its opposite. Suppose performance targets are explicit and payments are made *only* in response to the assessment of performance. We can skip case (ii) for present purposes. Now in case (i), under which effort is the same, prices and output remain the same and the results are similar to before. But suppose following case (iii) that effort fails. In this case the payments to employees are proportionately less. The price per unit of each commodity may remain the same, since at a lower effort level proportionately more hours of work per good is required, but the total value of goods produced is lower. But this is proportionate to the lower income received for effort by employees. Hence no goods need remain unsold, assuming that the propensity to consume remains the same. The contrast between this case and the previous one is unusually striking. The same goods are produced in two cases. The same behavioural rules are followed in the two cases. But the fixed versus the variable aspects of the contracts are quite different and the result is that in the former case inflation results, while in the latter case prices remain stable. Thus the nature of the contract matters a great deal.

It would be of interest, but it is difficult to consider, the case that is the exact obverse of the previous one – namely, the case in which performance is explicit but payment is variable and not dependent on performance. There are such cases, but the nature of these cases is rarely sufficiently widespread to be of general interest. For example, the custom of 'tipping' after performance is a case in point. Some identical services are offered at variable prices in the interest of discrimination, but buyers may have a choice under which discriminatory category they fall. For example, air travel is frequently of this nature. Suppose all contracts were of this nature, what would follow? The first two possibilities lead to the same results as before. The firm can reduce the rate of pay for the same performance, or pay the same as before. The outcomes are similar to the previous case under which we assumed that the explicit part of the contract was the monetary payment. The third possibility, under which there is an increase in return for effort, is also symmetrical, although at first it may be difficult to see why firms might want to behave in this way. But this is somewhat less mysterious if firms use a cost-plus percentage mark-up system of pricing.

While symmetrical results are obtainable in the case considered above, it must be self-evident that the previous type of contract is the more likely of the two − i.e. the contract in which the money payment is explicit but the effort level is not. General observation and experience suggests that this is the major type of contract extant for the most part in nonagricultural sectors. To the extent that we shall be concerned with developing countries, we shall be concerned primarily with their nonagricultural sectors.

III.   The Increasing Performance Case

Let us return for a moment to a case we touched on earlier. Money payment is explicit and effort is variable. Effort increases and cost per unit falls. We assumed before that firms use the same price formula for all three cases, and that prices fall. But is such symmetry warranted? May not firms retain the same price as before and indirectly allow profits per unit to rise? No inflationary effect is apparent, but all goods produced cannot be sold under these circumstances. We shall see later that if we introduce the concept of inert areas the behaviour just described is likely. This would suggest that if in some parts of an economy effort increases and in other parts effort declines, the overall effect is inflationary even if the average level of effort remains constant. We shall see that this type of argument can be bolstered when we introduce relative bargaining considerations.

IV.   Why Contracts Are Incomplete

Contracts may be either explicit or implicit, complete or incomplete. It is important to note that the considerations treated do not depend on the distinction between explicitness versus implicitness. Whether a contract is written or oral, is not the basic issue. While those elements which involve degrees of explicitness may influence the extent to which there is a meeting of the minds by the parties to the contract, and further it may determine the litigation that arises out of a contract, all of these matters are not the essence of the argument. The essence of the argument depends on two elements. (i) The interesting production units, especially of urban economies, are firms that have an indefinite life ahead of them, and (ii) the basic intra-firm co-operation relation is an indefinite employment relation. Incompleteness arises not only out of lack of explicitness in the employment relation, but also because by its very nature complete specification of what the employee is expected to do is impossible — some aspects of the contract must be left incomplete because it is factually impossible to do so, or because it is too expensive for the firm to try to do so, and to monitor the results.

In due course individual employees will acquire more local information about the nature of their job, and the possible options involved in carrying it out, than is available to any supervisor. Thus employees are usually in a position to use their discretion, if they wish to, and if they are allowed to, in carrying out their jobs. Hence the incompleteness of employment contracts depends more on the need to submit to a fact of life rather than a matter of convention. It is precisely because of such incompleteness, that firms are required to possess within their organisation authority relations which to some degree are substitutes for the lack of explicitness and *completeness* in the employment relation. However, authority relations are imperfect substitutes for incompleteness. Such authority relations cannot eliminate some degree of discretion available to employees in performance − i.e. in the determination of the nature and degree of effort that each employee puts into his job.

However, the implicit aspects of some contracts do affect the type of situations with which we are concerned. For example, consider the vague and 'implicit' contracts between buyers and sellers of a consumer's good who have daily or weekly transactions. Strictly speaking, each day may be viewed as involving a new contract unrelated to the prices of the previous day. But suppose that for a long time a given price holds. The buyer naturally develops the expectation that the price will remain the same and makes his plans accordingly. The seller may frequently welcome the development of such expectations since it may in a loose way 'tie' the buyer to a specific seller. Such implicit expectations involve considerable economies of information gathering. The seller does not have to appeal to all buyers each day, and the buyer does not have to canvas all possible sellers to see if he can do any better. To canvas all sellers on all possible transaction occasions is an impossibly costly activity for most buyers. Steady buyers will usually also expect that sellers will be implicitly 'fair' − i.e. that if other sellers reduce the price that his seller will do likewise.

Now, in view of the above, let us return to our previous example under which effort is gradually increased, and costs gradually fall; will such reductions in cost be passed on to consumers? The seller is keeping to his implicit aspect of the contract with his customer by keeping prices constant. The seller is also keeping to the *explicit* part of his contract with employees by paying them the agreed-upon wage. There is clearly no strong incentive for sellers to reduce prices to consumers. Consider also that the reduction in costs through an increase in effort is largely an invisible phenomenon. On the other hand changes in price are visible. Thus, for a considerable time, anyhow, there may be no way of buyers ever knowing that they have any reason whatsoever to expect lower prices or any 'claim' to receive lower prices. Hence, especially in view of our theory of *inert areas*, there is every reason to expect that prices will not be lowered, at least for some time, in the circumstances considered.

In the analysis developed thus far there appears to be an interesting asymmetry. There is a tendency for increase in cost to lead to higher prices, but in cases where there are reductions in cost, there is no equal set of forces that leads directly to lower prices. The *directness* of the price changes is worth considering carefully. We have seen that a mark-up pricing system leads to a direct translation of increased costs into increased prices on the part of the firms that experience the increase in costs. There is no similar direct change when there is a decrease in costs since there is no incentive on the part of firms to lower prices. This is not to say that lower prices cannot occur, but simply that there is an asymmetry (i) in the way in which it occurs, and (ii) in the speed with which it occurs, if it occurs at all. We shall also argue that there is similarly an asymmetry as to whether or not price reductions occur.

Several processes come to mind which could possibly lead to price declines. We might expect that some firms would perceive the lower costs as an opportunity to expand output, using the lower costs and lower prices as a means of attaining a greater market share. There are two important elements to be noted here. In the first place, the expansion of output requires organisational effort as well as additional resources. No successful organisational efforts or additional risks are required simply to increase price in the case of rising costs. Second, expanding output involves some risk. It increases the degree of competitiveness in the industry, upsets expected arrangements, and induces other firms to lower their prices. Thus firms contemplating expansion may visualise the entire procedure and decide that, since other firms are induced to lower their prices, they may not be better off at the end of the process than they were prior to the expansion.

A second approach is to note that lower costs should result in higher profit rates, which in turn should induce entrepreneurs to enter the high profit industry. However, entrepreneurs should anticipate the same process which a firm contemplating expansion would anticipate — i.e. entry into the industry would increase supply and lower prices and profits.

An aspect on the other side of the picture (the nonreduction of prices) that should be considered, is that firm members within the firm may see the increased profits as an opportunity for them to bargain for an increased share of the firm's revenues. Those with somewhat greater bargaining power are likely to be the first ones to attempt to achieve a redistribution of the firm's income in their favour. Those who do so may be either part of the official management, or part of the labour groups that happen to have, for one reason or another, more bargaining power than other groups. This is by no means the end of this aspect of the story. Once one group in the firm receives a higher return for its efforts, similar groups in other firms may do likewise. Increased wages in one industry may influence wages in other industries, so that parallel groups in those industries are likely to bargain for increased wage rates. To the extent that the latter are successful, they raise costs in their firms which in turn, using the cost-mark-up pricing formula, will result in higher prices in their industry. In this particular scenario we obtain the curious result that both increases in cost, *as well as decrease in cost*, result in higher prices.

All of this is not to argue that some reductions in cost, and some level of profit increases will not yield expansions and/or entries, and eventually lower prices. It is a matter of degree and we should not expect this result to occur in all circumstances.

In fact, we should expect that the outcome will depend on the relative propensity of entrepreneurs to enter the industry (for existing firms to expand), and the propensity for groups within the firm to be able to bargain successfully for a larger share of the firm's revenues. Suppose that the firm's inert areas with respect to prices are fairly large. As a result the firm initially maintains prices despite decreasing costs. And further suppose that there are some groups within the firm that have significant bargaining power with respect to revenues whose inert areas with respect to revenues are relatively small. Finally, assume that the inert areas for entrepreneurs with respect to entry are fairly large so that they enter at significant profit rate differentials. All of these assumptions are not at all inconceivable in many instances and they are especially likely to hold in developing countries in which there may be 'entrepreneur scarcities'. The outcome in this case will be as we have indicated in the previous paragraph. Thus the results depend both on the nature of inert areas on differential bargaining strength within the firm, and on the supply of entrepreneurs and the nature of their inert areas.

7 BARGAINING

I. Introduction

We considered in the previous chapter how different types of contracts, combined with some simple assumptions about employee and firm behaviour, might lead to inflationary pressures. However, we did not consider how the terms of the contract were arrived at — we simply assumed those terms for the explicit or complete parts of the contract. We now turn to the determination of contract terms. This can be a rather complex subject and a large volume would be required to handle it with any degree of thoroughness. However, some of the more salient points can be made with considerable brevity.

Let us begin with bargaining implications of conventional microtheory. We immediately run into a serious difficulty. Modern microtheory does not spell out the bargaining assumptions underlying it. The reason most probably is that for a discussion of comparative equilibria such a specification is unnecessary. The assumption of costless perfect market knowledge appears to make such a specification unnecessary. Basically what is assumed is multilateral renegotiable 'most favoured treatment' bargaining. Everyone gets to know everyone else's offer terms, assumes that the terms offered are the same to each individual, and every individual is then in a position to make his optimum deal. Bargaining in the sense of a process of negotiation is never assumed to take place. Differential bargaining skill or bargaining power does not enter into the theory. Of course, real contracts are arrived at through processes that are considerably more complex bargaining matters.

II.   Take It or Leave It (Tili) Bargaining Versus Negotiation Bargaining

There are various ways of suggesting the range of bargaining procedures. One way of doing so is indicated in Table 7.1. We shall not bother to go through all the possible permutations and combinations of bargaining means, bargains worked out, and their reactions between the two. First, for reasons explained in the last chapter, we shall not be concerned with complete contracts (except in passing), but shall focus our attention on incomplete contracts. Second, whether a bargain is strictly speaking a *one* item bargain or an *all* item bargain, is really immaterial. In other words, whether the *bundle* of contract items bargained over involves only *one* item, or is a *many* item bundle is immaterial as long as the bargaining is over the entire bundle. This is to be sharply distinguished from many item bargaining under which individuals trade off the terms of some items for others.

Let us start our discussion and consideration with bilateral bargaining. Irrespective of the environment, assume that only a buyer and a seller are involved. Consider at first the simplest case under which there is only one term of the contract to be bargained, say the money price for whatever it *is* that is traded. In the light of our previous discussions the reader must keep in mind the possibility that the 'item' traded is not necessarily perfectly specified. Thus, if the item traded is a service, not every particular aspect of the service need be specified in advance and completely known. For present purposes the only negotiable part of the contract is price. The simplest arrangement frequently experienced by many buyers is the one-sided 'take it or leave it' offer. The seller sets the price and the buyer is given the choice of accepting the price or not engaging in trade. There are considerable virtues to such bargaining arrangements *if one can afford them*; they save time and the emotional wear and tear of haggling! (Of course for some the process of haggling may be fun.)

Table 7.1

Type of Bargaining	One or Both Sides	One Item	All Items	Term Trade Offers	Some Items	Complete Contract	Incomplete Contract
BILATERAL							
a. Take it or leave it	One		X	X	X		X
Take it or leave it	Both		X	X	X		X
b. Negotiate							
(i) Offer terms	One		X	X	X		X
(ii) Offer terms	Both		X	X	X		X
c. Negotiate	Equal strength		X	X	X		X
Negotiate	Unequal strength		X	X	X		X
MULTILATERAL							
a. Auctions	Equal strength		X	X	X		X
Auctions	Unequal strength		X	X	X		X
b. Auctions — discriminatory			X	X	X		X
Auctions — nondiscriminatory			X	X	X		X
Multilateral individual			X	X	X		X

The opposite of 'take it or leave it' bargaining is bilateral negotiation. Why should economic agents employ take it or leave it bargaining over negotiation? A full benefit-cost analysis of these competing strategies would shed some light on the process. Part of the answer is clear (no general answer exists); the strategy used depends on specific circumstances. For example, in highly developed economies take it or leave it or 'one price' strategies will exist for small items, say groceries in a supermarket, but not for large, highly valuable items such as houses or automobiles. One general reason for this quickly comes to mind; individual item negotiation is costly in time, and negotiation costs are too expensive for small items, but it may be worth it for large ones.

But what advantages does negotiation yield even for large items? For one thing it may yield information about the degrees of desire of each party to trade. Obviously for the seller, the more eager the buyer, the higher the price. It is in the interest of each party to the potential transaction to disguise his eagerness to engage in the transaction. However the disguise must not be carried too far or else a transaction that both parties desire, or one which involves a gain for both parties, may fail to take place. Thus while for some the negotiation process may possess elements of a poker game, and be enjoyable for that reason, for others quite the opposite may be the case. They may feel that they are not especially gifted or skilled to engage in such negotiations and prefer a take it or leave it arrangement. In fact some of the opprobrium that has been attached to traders in some cultures may arise from the fact that negotiated trade allows for guile, and gain from the use of guile. Some may resent the fact that there is an advantage to be gained by being able to mislead the other party.

Another aspect of negotiated trade is the advantage attached to differences in information. In other words, if A has more information than B about the nature of the market, the product, or alternative possibilities of obtaining the product, then A can take advantage of this fact. Consider the situation under which A and B have equal access to all the pertinent information, but it takes time to collect the information, and hence A can take advantage of B's haste and as a consequence try and probably obtain a better price in the transaction than could otherwise be the case. Suppose that after the transaction is completed B discovers that this in fact has happened. B may feel that he has been cheated and resent the outcome. Of course it may be argued that B has no valid cause for complaint since he could have used more time and avoided the outcome. B traded a higher price for a little more leisure. But this argument about how A *should* feel or reason is really beside the point in my view. What matters from the point of view of analysis is how B actually feels for the purposes of the analysis of the situation. In other words, B may have a taste for avoiding the type of 'unfair' outcomes that detailed negotiated trading can lead to. Thus sellers that offer take it or leave it price contracts (plus the implication that everyone gets the same deal) do cater to a specific want. In fact markets may split up on this basis. One finds in some cities, especially in developing countries, that some portions of the city, or some establishments, will sell only on a single price, take it or leave it basis, while other sections may contain 'bazaars' or other establishments in which 'bargaining' or 'haggling' over price is customary.

We should by no means conclude from the above that single price (take it or leave it) offers are in fact in any real, ethical or other sense 'fairer' than negotiated pricing. A monopolist using a single price formula may in a sense be fleecing everybody but doing it equally. Nevertheless there are certain time and taste costs which are avoided by single price, take it or leave it bargaining systems.

III. Comments on the Theory of Bargaining

Before proceeding further it may be useful to consider very briefly the literature on bargaining theory and bargaining power as developed by economists. Two of the earliest theories are those developed by Zeuthen[1] and Hicks.[2] For simplicity it may be helpful if we begin with a brief statement of the theory developed by Hicks, and then proceed to Zeuthen and others. The virtue of Hicks's theory of bargaining is that it is exceedingly simple and hence it is easy to see what the theory attempts to say. The bargaining in Hicks is between a trade union and an employer, and the cost of bargaining is determined by the length of a strike expected. Using what are clearly analogues of demand and supply analysis, Hicks postulates the existence of an *employer's concession curve*, which depends on the length of the strike, and the *union's resistance curve*. Up to a point, the greater the length of a strike expected, the greater the increase in wages the employer is willing to concede. From the union's viewpoint the greater the length of a strike the smaller the wage rate the union is willing to accept. The intersection of these two curves determines the wage-rate increase that would be acceptable to both the employer and the union. This is the normal partial equilibrium analysis. It is illustrated in Figure 7.1.

From the point of view of this study, it is worth noting several aspects about Hicks's simple theory. In the first place, in the Hicksian model there is no 'nontransaction' risk. This could readily be inserted into the model, but it would normally be presumed that there is no such risk given the nature of the entities engaged in the bargaining; if the employer does not consider one of the serious options which is to close down the plant, then the employees do not consider their option to leave the employer simultaneously as a group. This is one of the deficiencies of labour-management bargaining models if we seek to generalise them to other bargaining areas.

On the positive side, Hicks's model has the virtue of being implicitly a bargaining power model. Here the bargaining power can quite clearly be translated as the capacity to impose a serious cost on the other party.

Figure 7.1

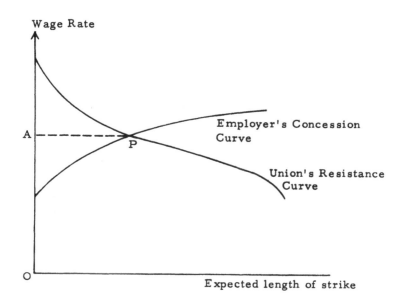

Zeuthen's model is somewhat more general, but in some respects it is similar. Zeuthen considers that the major element is the *risk* of conflict. This might be defined as the probability of having to endure the strike cost. Zeuthen's model seems to argue that there is a value of the probability risk of conflict which determines the intersection of the gains and losses for both parties.

While it is not possible to equate the Zeuthen and Hicks models, it is possible to work out a combined model which indicates the contribution that each makes. One such combined model could be developed simply by discounting the gains and the losses in each of the models by some risk of conflict. Thus, in the Hicks model, both the increase in wages and the costs of a strike would be discounted by a probabilistic risk factor. Similarly, in the Zeuthen model we would discount the gains and the losses of each party to the negotiations.[3]

The model developed by the Dutch economist, Pen,[4] is

somewhat similar to Zeuthen's model. There is an implicit
discounting process, which is the subjective probability of the
risk conflict, and its inverse, the risk of nonconflict, i.e.
$1 - r$ where r is the risk of conflict). Pen, however, introduced one additional element which is of special interest;
namely the fact that in bargaining between buyers and sellers
it is of interest to one or both parties involved to conceal
their subjective evaluation of the risk. Thus Pen explicitly
includes the subjective evaluation to one or both parties of
ending up with a nontransaction.

These brief remarks do not present the theories in all of
their richness and subtlety, and they certainly do not do
justice to their intellectual content. More recently, a number
of additional theories have been developed along the lines of
Hicks, Zeuthen and others, and a considerable debate has
developed in the literature about the significance and rele-
vance of the various models. For instance, the Hicksian
model has been criticised by some and defended by others.[5]
However, for present purposes, we need not go into the
details of the various debates since they deal mostly with
issues that are not significant for this essay. For an understanding of the relation between bargaining power and inflation, it is not necessary for us to have a detailed, specific
workable model that will predict accurately in specific
negotiation or instances of haggling.

One of the most interesting analyses of bargaining power
is that developed by Thomas Schelling.[6] Schelling points out
that what may appear as a source of bargaining strength, in
actual negotiation may turn out to be a weakness and vice
versa. For instance, it is frequently believed that the individual with greater resources will have greater bargaining
power. However, according to Schelling, there are many
instances in which this cannot be translated into a bargaining
advantage, but rather it becomes a bargaining disadvantage.
Consider the case of a rich man and a relatively poor man,
each of whom may wish to buy the same house whose value
is believed to be approximately $20,000. The poor man can

afford no more than $ 16,000. This is clear to the seller. The rich man wishes to pay no more than $ 16,000, but it is clear to the seller that he could afford more. The rich man has alternatives that the poor man does not. However, if the rich man were the only buyer, he would have considerable difficulty in obtaining the house for only $ 16,000. He could not claim that he could not pay a higher price. Because of the seller's knowledge of his wealth, he would probably have to come much closer to the seller's asking price if he wanted the transaction to be consummated. If the poor man were the only potential buyer he could obtain it for $ 16,000, since the seller would not want to forgo the benefits of a transaction, and he knows the poor man cannot go any higher. Schelling specifies a number of other examples where apparent strength leads to the 'strong party' obtaining less of the difference between the buyer's and seller's limit prices than those with apparent weaknesses. The following quotation from Schelling's essay indicates the general nature of the argument involved.

> When a person — or a country — has lost the power to help himself, or the power to avert mutual damage, the other interested party has no choice but to assume the cost or responsibility. 'Coercive deficiency' is the term Arthur Smithies uses to describe the tactic of deliberately exhausting one's annual budgetary allowance so early in the year that the need for more funds is irresistibly urgent.[7]

It would seem to me, however, that a good deal of the discussion on bargaining misses an important distinction. That is, the distinction between bargaining power as a stock concept and bargaining capacity in special circumstances as a flow concept. The specific instances are part of the flow of transactions in which individuals have to engage in carrying out their activities. In other words, it is one thing to have bargaining power, it is something else to use it. The cost of using one's bargaining power may depend on specific

circumstances but the circumstances need not reflect general
bargaining power. This would be somewhat similar to confus-
ing the budgetary constraints (i.e. the income and wealth of
a household) possessed by a rich versus a poor family, as
against their behaviour in purchasing specific goods. It may
not pay for the rich man to haggle over the price of some
small item, whereas it may pay for the poor man to do so.
Nevertheless, should the rich man wish to haggle, since he has
many more alternatives than the poor man, he may be able
to do so more successfully than the poor man.

The view taken here is that bargaining power depends on
the alternatives available to an individual. The extent to
which the individual uses these alternatives depends on a
specific circumstance and may or may not involve the use of
all or any of the bargaining power that a person possesses.
We shall see that whether or not one uses one's bargaining
power will depend on the variety of factors which determine
bargaining power in the different markets in which a person
is *simultaneously* engaged. An additional factor that will turn
out to be significant is whether or not the individual will have
to absorb the adverse consequences of a given bargain, or
whether such consequences can be passed on to others in the
economy.

IV.   Take It or Leave It (Tili) Bargaining Continued

Another element in take it or leave it pricing is bargaining
power. Who can afford to make take it or leave it offers?
Everyone? Obviously not those who have no alternatives or
feel that they cannot afford the alternatives they have. Those
with limited skills in a tight labour market, whose alternative
is unemployment, cannot offer a take it or leave it wage
contract to a prospective employer. In fact such an individual is likely to find him or herself at the receiving end of a
take it or leave it offer. At the other extreme a clear-cut
monopolist can readily afford the luxury of offering take it

or leave it contracts. Whether the monopolist will do so may depend, in part, on taste and convention in the industry, and in part on whether he feels he can obtain more information in engaging in negotiations up to a point. After all, a true monopolist can always cut off negotiations and offer a take it or leave it contract at any point he chooses. Monopolists can obviously afford to offer such contracts.

What about the in-between cases. Those in clearly product-differentiated industries are also in a position to do so within limits. They hold partial monopolies for their version of the 'product' or product class, but buyers have alternative choices. There are fairly close substitutes depending on the nature of the product group and the tastes of the buyers. The only point being made is that sellers in such industries are in a position to do so, but they may not necessarily do so. Both monopolists and monopolistic competitors (differentiated product sellers) have discretion in this area. One more condition must be met. There must also be relatively many buyers. Essentially bilateral monopolists cannot carry out such a strategy. We consider this matter later.

Atomistic competition, with presumably little power on both sides, does not rule out the use of take it or leave it strategy. What matters is that there are many buyers and sellers so that each feels he has alternatives. If the initial price set is too high for adequate transactions to take place it can be lowered, but any specific buyer at any one time will still face a take it or leave it strategy.

Negotiated pricing is likely to take place under three sets of circumstances: (i) very thin markets, (ii) useful information obtainable in the negotiation process greater than the cost of negotiation, and (iii) a desire to maximise the gains from price discrimination. Clearly, if the market is very thin on both sides, each party is likely to feel that they should endeavour to determine if a mutually profitable transaction exists. The costs of failure are too great to risk a take it or leave it strategy. The circumstances of the second possibility are harder to specify. Someone in a weak bargaining position cannot insist on negotiation just because he may thereby garner useful information. Clearly, only if both parties feel that negotiation is informationally useful, or if the stronger party feels that this is the case, will negotiation take place. It is axiomatic that price discrimination can yield greater gains to the price discriminator than a single price for everyone. But price discrimination requires information on the resources and intensity of desire of potential buyers. Negotiation may (but need not necessarily do so) help reveal such information and hence price discrimination may resort to negotiation.

One possible misunderstanding of the previous discussion has to be cleared up. Take it or leave it bargaining does not necessarily imply simple price contracts where more than one party is involved. Take it or leave it bargain offers may just as readily be associated with price discrimination. If sellers make the take it or leave it offers, buyers may be divided into categories and given different take it or leave it offers. This is frequently the case in different types of transportation. There is generally a strong tendency to use this approach in industries in which there is a large differential between average and marginal costs of production. The problem usually faced by sellers of this type is to try to establish the categories in such a way so that individuals in one category find it difficult, if not impossible, to shift to economically more advantageous categories. Frequently what on the surface may appear as single price offers will allow for systematic or *ad hoc* discounts, so that in effect multiple price offers are really available. We shall examine this problem at various points as we continue our discussion of bargaining since sellers may wish to offer take it or leave it offers to weak bargainers, but allow for negotiated terms with strong bargainers.

Why should we care about take it or leave it offers and contracts? We shall see that there are circumstances under which these types of offers can and do play a major role in the inflationary process. But there are additional considerations for our concern. As a shorthand let us refer to 'take it or leave it' offers by their initials – *Tili* offers.

To begin with, in imperfect markets, Tili offers, on one or both sides, are unlikely to maximise transactions. In the absence of perfect knowledge, or negotiation processes that reveal such knowledge, Tili price offers may be set too high for some or many buyers. In other words, there may be mutually advantageous transactions that could be missed because the Tili type of offer does not allow for sufficient probing of the market. During periods when other economic conditions result in full employment this may not be very important. But under less than full employment this may be important. That is, under less than full employment such practices may contribute to the continuation of the level of unemployment. Under negotiation there is at least a chance that a seller (who would otherwise have a take it or leave it offer) could discover that his Tili price is too high for a transaction, but under the take it or leave it procedures the seller may have no way of discovering this. Suppose that the Tili price is simply a price that is posted somewhere. The seller posting the price does not know how many of those who do not respond to the posted price would not have responded in any event, and how many would have responded to a lower price. Clearly, negotiation might have revealed some of the lower price responders. (This is an area in which experiments might lead to interesting findings.)

The lack of negotiation that accompanies many Tili offers can lead to less information about the 'product' than would otherwise be the case, and less information than is desirable on welfare economic grounds. This is not to argue that this will be the case universally. Whether or not this turns out to be the case will depend on circumstances. The main point is to alert the reader to this possibility. Such outcomes are especially likely in circumstances under which the one making the Tili offer is in a strong bargaining position, while the other party is in a relatively weak one.

V. Tili Offers and Inflation

Tili offers are especially likely to accommodate inflationary processes when we take into account our inert area hypothesis. If sellers make Tili offers, and over time these offers involve gradually rising prices, such prices may be readily absorbed by 'buyers' since the price increases are not strong enough to go beyond the inert areas of buyers. In other words, the inert areas may be smaller if prices are negotiated rather than on a Tili basis. Why? There may be an attention-getting aspect to negotiation that does not always exist (at least to the same degree) for (at least) routine Tili offers. To the extent that the inert area contains an 'impact realisation' component, the inert areas may be smaller under negotiated prices. Or, put another way, negotiation has a greater impact realisation effect than Tili offers. Hence Tili price offers may be more readily absorbed, while negotiation may more readily lead to some voiced resistance.

An important type of take it or leave it price offer occurs where bureaucratic organisations are involved. One or both parties to the transaction may be *agents* of bureaucracies, rather than *principals*. If both parties are agents they may have very little incentive to bargain over price. At least not to bargain as strongly as their *principals* would. In the case in which one party is a bureaucracy (whether private or public), and the bureaucracy makes a Tili offer, it may be impossible for most buyers to even try to negotiate were they inclined to do so. Thus bureaucratic Tili offers may be less subject to any type of reasonable adjustment, or show responsiveness to bargaining, than would take place if the economic agents involved were individuals or small firms. In other words, bureaucratic procedures may preclude detailed bargaining in many instances.

In any event, bargaining between agents is not the same as bargaining between principals. This is essentially the case if the principals are groups rather than individuals. The reason for this is that bargaining by principals is simpler. Not only do agents sometimes have to refer back to their principals, but they also have different motives. That is, agents' motives are usually mixed. They have their own personal interests (say, careerist interests) to satisfy as well as their conception of the interests of the principals; agents are unlikely to *feel* the interests of their principals as keenly as the principals themselves. Unfortunately it is rather difficult to generalise about the way in which agent bargaining differs from that of their principals. A great deal will depend on how the agents view their jobs. Consider the case in which the agent seller views his job interpretation as one that emphasises price — the higher the price, the more he feels he will gain his principal's approval. On the other side, suppose the agent buyer's job interpretation emphasises completing transactions. Clearly, under the hypothesised circumstances the agent buyer will not bargain very hard over price. There are many other combinations of job interpretation emphasis, some of which would lead to the opposite result of those just indicated.

Let us return to our original question. Why are we interested in Tili contract offers? The reason is that they yield to certain individuals or firms various degrees of price-setting power, and to some degree, the capacity to pass on price increases to others. This may result from bargaining power superiority. But these are not the only circumstances. Highly entrenched conventions in certain professions may yield to the same result. In any event we have seen, through the consideration of various hypothetical examples, that the analysis of such offers can lead to insights into the circumstances under which contract types allow some economic agents to pass on price increases to others. The point of the discussion of the various types taken should emerge in the last chapter, where various elements will be combined and their implications indicated. However, it may be helpful at this point to suggest briefly the motivation behind our discussion of bargaining and contracts to the extent that we have considered them.

Let us recall that we argue that the payments part of the contract is likely to be explicit, whereas the performance part is likely to be an incomplete element of the employment contract. Bargaining, for the most part, is likely to involve the payments aspect, rather than performance. Now the significance of bargaining power, combined with take it or leave it price offers can result in price-setting power. The existence of price-setting power, in an economy combined with inert areas, allows some firms to raise prices (to some degree) without undue concern about the response. This is especially likely to be the case if the response cannot be voiced but could only be reflected in exit.[8] This in turn can lead to a leap-frogging process in which some firms raise prices in an attempt to either increase revenue, or in response to increases in input prices, which in turn leads others with some degree of similar power to increase their prices, while input owners with bargaining power try to increase their prices, and so on. Since not all groups have the same degree of bargaining power, and their inert areas are of different sizes and imply differential degrees of responsiveness, this can lead to a process in which there are sequential responses over time. Those who are late in the process, or do not have the bargaining power to enter it, will lose (at least temporarily) as prices generally rise around them. Thus we see that there is a possible connection between the ideas discussed, their contribution to the process of inflation, and their impact on income distribution. Especially interesting are those cases in which relatively vulnerable individuals in the society are also those with very little bargaining power.

Notes

1. F. Zeuthen, *Problems of Monopoly and Economic Warfare* (Routledge and Kegan Paul Ltd, London, 1930).

2. J.R Hicks, *The Theory of Wages* (Macmillan, New York, 1932).

3. See the article by Robert L. Bishop, 'A Zeuthen-Hicks Theory of Bargaining', *Econometrics*, vol. 32, no. 3 (July 1964), pp. 410-17. One has to distinguish between the discount factor due to risk and one which explicitly takes timing into account. The latter may take into account the time involved in the flow of gains and losses. An additional element, where appropriate, is the *holding out* time. That is, some individuals may find it possible to hold out before accepting an offer for a longer period than others. Bishop's model emphasises this latter point. An additional element is the probability that different bargaining agents may have different subjective rates of discount. For an interesting survey of most of this literature see Alan Coddington, *Theories of the Bargaining Process* (George Allen and Unwin Ltd, London, 1968), pp. 24-48.

4. Jan Pen, 'A General Theory of Bargaining', *American Economic Review*, vol. 42 (March 1952).

5. See, G.L.S. Shackle, 'The Nature of the Bargaining Process', Chapter 19 in *The Theory of Wage Determination*, John T. Dunlop, ed. (Macmillan, London, 1957); J. Johnston, 'A Model of Wage Determination Under Bilateral Monopoly', *Economic Journal* (September 1972).

6. Thomas C. Schelling, *The Strategy of Conflict* (Oxford University Press, New York, 1963), pp. 21-53.

7. Ibid., p. 37.

8. In this area it is of interest to consider Albert A. Hirschman's discussion of 'Voice' versus 'exit', although Hirschman does not explicitly apply it to the inflation problems.

8 MULTIPLE POSITION BARGAINING ANALYSIS

I. Multiple Bargaining Power Positions

Thus far we have considered the bargaining problem only from the viewpoint of a single market. We now have to treat the problem from a more complex but more realistic viewpoint. Individuals, households and firms are usually in at least two markets simultaneously, as buyers in one set of markets and sellers in another. Thus, adults are usually sellers or potential sellers in one or more labour markets, and buyers in a number of consumer markets. Similarly, firms are buyers of inputs in one set of markets and sellers of goods in others. This is all elementary. But the next step is not elementary and is rarely treated. Economic actors may be weak in some markets and strong in others, or weak in all markets, or possibly, in rare cases, strong in all markets. How is bargaining affected by the fact that individuals are in multiple markets and possess different degrees of bargaining strength in them? Will an individual who is weak in one market and strong in another behave differently than the one who is weak in both? Does it matter if two bargainers are symmetrical or antisymmetrical in their multiple market position?

We assume that every economic actor is in two markets, one in which he is a buyer and the other a seller. Thus, in Figure 8.1, the legend WS means that the economic actor is weak in his *buyers* market and *strong* in his sellers market. The other initials indicate similar meaning.

In Figure 8.1 W = weak and S = strong. Let the first letter indicate the position in the market in which he is not bargaining. Thus, WS/WS indicates a buyer and seller facing each other, both of whom are strong in the market in which they are bargaining and weak in their other market. If this is a

Figure 8.1

Seller Buyers	WW	WS	SW	SS
WW	E			
WS	W/S	E		
SW	W/S	E/A	E	
SS	W/S	W/SA	W/SA	E

Legend: E = equal bargaining power; W/S = weak versus strong;
E/A = equal – asymmetrical; W/SA = weak versus strong asymmetrical.

commodity market then the buyer may be weak as a seller of labour, and the seller is weak as a buyer of inputs. Bargains struck in such markets are rather indeterminate – they are likely to be rather neutral as a source of transmitting inflationary pressure.

Although the 4 × 4 table allows for 16 possible cases, it is not necessary to analyse all of them, since symmetrical cases are formally likely to yield the same results. Thus, the outcome of WS/WW is similar to the outcome of WW/WS. Thus, the cases to be considered are: (I) those along the diagonal – (1) WW/WW, (2) WS/WS, (3) SW/SW and (4) SS/SS; and (II) the six nonsymmetrical cases off the diagonal – (5) WW/WS, (6) WW/SW, (7) WW/SS, (8) WS/SW, (9) WS/SS and (10) SW/SS.

Now the cases along the diagonal involve bargaining between people in similar circumstances. They are all cases in which bargainers have equal bargaining power *vis-à-vis* each other but not necessarily against each other. But symmetry allows us to simplify the analysis. For the most part we can safely concentrate on the six cases off the diagonal.

Off the diagonal there is one interesting and overwhelmingly important characteristic that all the cases possess. In all of the cases there is one market in which one of the parties is strong and the other weak.

Weak vs strong cases	*Some strength for both parties*
(1) WW/SW	(4) SW/WS
(2) WW/SS	(5) SW/SS
(3) WW/WS	(6) WS/SS

Of great interest is that one of the parties in half of the cases is weak in both of his markets. Obviously such parties engaged in bargaining have very little room to manoeuvre. They cannot make up their weakness in one market by taking advantage of their strength in the other. Furthermore they face opposing bargainers who have some strength. Hence they must lose in one market and perhaps in both. Thus, to the extent that bargaining plays a role in determining the gains and losses from inflation, the ones who are weak in both markets are bound to lose in the process. Here we have a clear-cut result. We shall return to this category of cases.

Case (4) is especially interesting. These bargainers can come out even in the inflation process – but not with respect to each other. That is, they come out even in *real terms* and do not stay the same. To the extent that they lose by rising money prices in their weak market, they can score counterpart money gains in their strong market. Thus money prices rise but the real distribution of income does not change.

In the final two cases, one party is strong in both markets while the other is not. Clearly, the party that is not strong in both markets must lose in terms of real income distribution. What about the process? The strong party in both markets has no real incentive to fight rising money prices in the market in which he is strong (up to a point), since he can *more* than recoup in the market in which the other is weak.

At this juncture it is appropriate to consider in greater detail the process through which we would expect the various wage and price changes to occur. In other words, we examine how various combinations of bargaining strength and bargaining weakness translate themselves into changes in wages and prices. First consider the case in which take it or leave it offers are involved, and in which case (6), WS/SS, is under consideration. That is, suppose that party A is weak in one market and strong in the other, and B is strong in both markets. If A represents workers who are weak in the consumer market but strong in the labour market through, let us say, a trade union, then we can visualise the trade union making a take it or leave it offer to firm B. Firm B does have the capacity to refuse the offer and fight the trade union to achieve a lower wage. However, since the firm is strong in its other market, say the market in which it sells its goods, it does not have a strong incentive to resist the take it or leave it offer. After all, it could always pass on the increase in costs to its strong market – assuming consumers are weak in that market. This is an interesting variation of the Schelling bargaining thesis. That is, even in the case in which both parties are strong, it may nevertheless pay for one of the parties not to resist the attempt to gain by the other party.

A variant of the process discussed above is one in which there is negotiation in the input market but party B sets prices on a take it or leave it basis in the commodity market. In this case, party B does not have an exceptionally strong incentive to negotiate as effectively as he could since he has price-setting powers in the commodity market. The result may be similar even in the case in which one party is weak in both markets and the other party is strong in one market – one in which he has price-setting power. Despite the relative weakness of party A in both markets, he may nevertheless prevail in obtaining an increase in wages if these wages could be passed on in B's strong market. The main idea that emerges in considering multiple markets simultaneously is that strength in some markets may counteract weaknesses in others. Equally important, it may result in strength not being used in one market if there is strength in some other markets. Thus firms or bargaining agents who are strong in more than one market will not necessarily resist demands for increased wages or increased prices if they find it convenient to shift burdens of such demands to other markets. This last argument presumes that in some sense there is a real cost or a utility cost in resisting increased price or wage demands even in markets in which the bargaining agent may be strong.

Will bargainers resist rising money prices? Only if they are not sufficiently strong compared to opposing bargainers in some other market to make up for the losses, if any. The main point of all of this is (i) that *there* are a greater many cases that some individuals are not in, in which there is no interest to fight inflation; and (ii) those who do have an interest to fight inflation are in a weak bargaining position. There is not much they can do about it. What they can try to do is get into a strong bargaining position *vis-à-vis* others. To the extent that they succeed, they put others in a weak bargaining position.

The upshot of all this is that unless we put everyone in a symmetrical bargaining position (that is, the WW/WW, and SS/SS positions on a diagonal), there will be a tendency for inflationary pressures except in cases of extreme monetary restrictions and cash flow deficiencies *and*/or considerable unemployment. (The latter can be interpreted to mean the same thing – namely extreme cash flow deficiencies in households.)

These conclusions may be seen more readily if they are restated in a somewhat different way. First there are basically two classes of bargaining situations: (i) symmetrical, and (ii) nonsymmetrical. Referring to our diagram the symmetrical situations are those on the top-left-bottom-right diagonal. In this set of cases the contending parties are in each case equally matched in terms of strength or weakness. Hence their real position does not worsen in bargaining. Second, in all other cases bargaining power is unequal. Some are stronger than others in some markets. These can gain in that market and can raise prices in that market — in some cases to make up for losses in the other market. In the second sub-group one party is weak in both markets and they lose as the stronger ones raise prices.

Now let us look at the case on the diagonal. Since the contending parties are of equal strength, they cannot gain *vis-à-vis* each other in real terms. However, it does not follow that they cannot contribute to inflation in many circumstances. If both parties are weak (WW/WW) in both markets they are unlikely to raise prices *vis-à-vis* each other. However, consider the cases WS/WS and SS/SS. In the WS/WS case, although both are strong *vis-à-vis* each other, they may nevertheless raise money prices to make up for money price increases in markets in which they are weak *vis-à-vis* third parties. In the case in which both parties are strong (SS/SS), they may raise prices in third markets, if such exist in which they are not contending with each other, and in which others are weak. If there are no such third markets then this case is either similar to the WW/WW case, or nondefinable in these terms, since strength and weakness are relative terms and not absolute terms.

II. Changing One's Bargaining Position

Thus far we have considered bargaining as if bargaining strength is fixed once and for all. But we have argued that bargaining depends on alternatives, and viable alternatives are not fixed once and for all, for all individuals. Indeed, for most individuals, in many instances viable alternatives depend on price. Consider individuals whose sole source of income is their job. (This is the case for most individuals.) Their viable alternative is likely to depend on the wage rate of their job *vis-à-vis* other jobs. In some jobs individuals may be weak in terms of their bargaining power but in other jobs to which they could move in terms of skill, labour's bargaining power may be strong. Thus, as inflation proceeds, individuals in jobs in which labour's bargaining position is weak will have an incentive to move to jobs in which labour is strong. Such moves are likely to operate as a counter income redistribution move, although at the same time it may increase the inflation process. In accordance with standard economic analysis, the move out of the 'weak' labour market will result in a tendency for money wages to rise in this market in order to attract back some of those who have left, or to attract individuals from other skills who are technically capable of handling the job in the strong labour market and who find that their position is becoming worse in real terms. As a consequence those in the strong market bargain for, and eventually receive, a money wage increase. Thus we can see in terms of this illustration a see-saw type of process in which one group falls behind in real terms and then catches up, while in its turn another group who was ahead falls behind — but at the same time money wages and prices keep going up in order to carry out the see-saw type of adjustments which take place.

What role do inert areas play in all this? Inert areas will play the usual expected role in the see-saw bargaining process. We would normally expect that those with narrower inert areas will move earlier out of industries in which their bargaining power is weak and into those in which it is strong. Similarly in the strong labour power industries, those with the narrowest inert areas will be the ones to bargain more aggressively for increased money wages. As labour scarcities affect the industries in which labour power is weak, their bargaining position should increase and normally, we would expect wage rates to rise. However, we do have to take into account the inert areas of the firms in the labour weak industries; so that despite scarcities there may be lags before these firms respond by making higher money wage offers. Thus on the whole the inert areas continue to permit the see-saw process to operate in the way one would expect on the basis of conventional theory. The existence of the inert areas introduces various degrees of sluggishness into the process. If, on the average, the inert areas in the labour weak industry are larger than the ones in the labour strong industry, then we would expect this to be an additional force in the falling behind of their real income as the inflation process proceeds. Alternately, we would expect the opposite to be the case if those in the labour strong industry are also the ones that contain the firms in which the inert areas are largest. It would seem difficult to say on a purely *a priori* basis whether on the average wide or narrow inert areas are more likely to be associated with labour weak as against labour strong bargaining power.

In our initial discussion of the see-saw bargaining process we implicitly assumed symmetrical movements in each direction and symmetrical changes in bargaining strength. Of course, this need not be the case. As individuals move from one industry to another they may change their rates of responsiveness both as a function of age, and as a result of relative tastes for security. Suppose most people prefer to be risk-averse with respect to inflationary losses. As a result, we might expect a gradual movement into the labour strong industry and a smaller movement out of it as wage differentials increase in favour of the labour weak industry. Thus, up to a point, inflation will cause more and more people to move towards the labour strong industries and two types of individuals will end up in the labour weak industry. These will be new workers, who might initially be attracted by the higher wages and are less concerned about security, and those in the labour weak industry who have so few alternatives that they cannot move to the labour strong one. This last group is not necessarily the most economically vulnerable group in society although it may contain a majority of such individuals.

Another group that may find itself especially vulnerable to inflation are those with a high degree of specialised training who, because of their specialisation, find that they are stuck in a given industry. Their alternatives may come into play if there are precipitous reductions in their relative real incomes. In other words, the extent to which an individual feels that his alternatives are viable will depend on (i) the return he obtains from a high degree of specialisation, and (ii) the fall in real wages which reduce these returns compared to other occupations for which he may be qualified.

III.   Survival Strategies in the Face of Inflation

Thus far we have been concerned entirely with the means through which inflation spreads as part of differential degrees of bargaining, and differential bargaining power. We have argued that the bargaining process, and the way in which contracts are made, will determine the transmission of inflationary pressure. In this section we will want to consider why there should be a gradual spread of 'take it or leave it' bargaining strategies and, at the same time, how individuals and firms should behave in the face of such strategies.

It is self-evident that the worse position to be in if one expects an inflationary process is to be relatively weak in all markets. In such a case the only counter to inflation is the existence of sufficient competition in some markets so that movement out of some markets into others can operate as a counter-inflationary tendency. Nevertheless, such movements are likely to be sluggish and as a result those who are weak in all markets may turn out to be not only short-run but also long-run losers in the inflationary process. The extreme case is those whose earnings depend on investments in which the return is of a fixed monetary value such as investors in ordinary bonds or contributors to various types of pension plans.

Firms may also find themselves relatively weak in many markets, or relatively weak on the average, so that they are vulnerable to inflationary pressures. For instance, some firms may find themselves being complete price takers in the markets for their inputs, and, simultaneously, to be almost price takers in the markets in which they sell their products. Now

suppose that the input market operates under greater inflationary pressures than the markets in which they sell, then
such firms will either face losses and eventual bankruptcy or
must put forth strenuous efforts to increase their X-efficiency. In terms of their overall bargaining power, in the
variety of markets in which they operate, such firms are in
a vulnerable position and it would seem natural for them to
try to change the market structure in at least some of the
markets in which they operate. Thus, they may attempt to
differentiate their product and obtain a partial monopolistic
position thereby, or they may attempt to enter into implicit
or explicit cartel arrangements, so that they could pass on
increased costs in some markets in the form of increased
prices in other markets without necessarily attempting to
improve the X-efficiency of their firm. In other words the
attainment of bargaining strength somewhere is a substitute
strategy for having to struggle against internal inefficiency
within the firm.

It can also be shown on the basis of examining the survival
mechanisms of firms that it is not necessarily the efficient
firms that survive. It may very well be that those who have or
develop strong bargaining positions have the greatest chance
of survival. We now turn to examine this argument in detail.
The survival of firms is usually threatened by two aspects,
lack of profitability or an inadequate cash flow. It is self-
evident that nonsubsidised private enterprise firms cannot
sustain losses indefinitely. Similarly, in the case of imperfect
capital markets, an inadequate cash flow will make it impossible for a firm to pay its debts in the short run, despite the
fact that in the long run it would be a profitable operation.
In the second case, regarding the conditions for assessment
of long-run profitability – the firm's self assessment may
differ from the banking institution from whom loans are
requested. The firm may assess its prospects quite accurately,
and they may indicate long-run profitability, while the
banking organisations, who may be using relatively short-run
arbitrary criteria for loans, may turn down loan requests of

long-run viable firms. In both cases profitability and cash flow may be assured if the firm has strong bargaining power in the seller's market so that they can raise prices and avoid losses to make up for a weak bargaining position in the input market, or to make up for increasing X-inefficiency.

Of course there are, up to a point, some constraining influences to arbitrary price increases. As relative prices rise, the elasticity of demand may increase according to the point at which the value of gross sales declines below its former level. However, we should keep in mind that with the type of analysis we are undertaking here, the elasticity of demand in terms of money prices does not remain constant for each price. If in the rest of the economy inflation is in progress, then for many commodities the elasticity of demand will rise at the same time as money prices rise.

Consider three cases: (i) positive growth in the macro sense, (ii) constant growth, and (iii) declines in real terms of net national product. In the first case, the increase in inputs may create positive growth level. The net result is a rise in real income, and firms with high bargaining power will have the capacity to raise prices as their efficiency declines and still be in a profitable position. Their overall demand need not decline since it will be compensated for by the increased demand, which is a consequence of the overall growth in real income.

The zero growth case is somewhat more complex. Here we are concerned with zero growth in real income and not money income and, hence, zero growth may be associated with net national income growth in current dollars (or whatever the currency under consideration happens to be). Clearly the firms with bargaining power may be able to raise prices to an extent greater than the inflation rate and increase profits at the expense of firms in highly competitive industries where strong competitive pressures do not allow firms to raise money prices. In the latter case consumers are presumed to have many alternatives and hence this minimises the possibility of any firm raising its price to compensate for an increase in X-inefficiency. A somewhat similar but less strong argument for the firms with bargaining power can also be made for the case in which net national income declines.

It is of special interest to show that we can visualise cases in which inefficient firms with bargaining power can survive, while relatively efficient firms without bargaining power would be forced out of business.

9   REVIEW AND POLICY IMPLICATIONS

In this chapter we summarise briefly the various ideas developed in the previous chapters, and consider some of the possible policy implications.

I.   Review of Essential Ideas

We have argued that in order to understand who gains and who loses as a consequence of inflation, we have to consider the set of bargaining positions that every economic actor faces. Each actor is involved in at least two markets simultaneously: as the buyer of some goods, and as a seller of inputs or other goods. At the very least, individuals in the workforce are buyers of consumer goods and sellers of labour skills. Other economic actors, either individuals or firms, may be involved in a multiplicity of markets. They may be strong in some markets and weak in others, or strong in all markets, or weak in all markets. In any event, to assess the impact of inflation we have to examine the relative strength in some markets versus the weakness in others faced by the same individuals.

To some degree those who are weak in some markets can make up for inflation losses if they are strong in other markets. In that case they are able to impose the inflationary losses on those who are weak where they are strong. Thus, by examining the relative multi-position bargaining strength of different individuals, we can trace the impact of inflation. In Chapter 6 we considered the various ways in which analyses of this type can be worked out.

In general we have argued that inflation distorts the development process for a given level of investment. Of course, it also distorts the distribution of income simultaneously. The

distortion takes place as a consequence of two basic considerations: (i) some goods offer more of a hedge against inflation
compared to others, and (ii) goods produced in some markets
allow for stronger market power (or bargaining power) than
in others. It is obviously advantageous to be able to shift out
of some markets and into others – usually from those in
which one's bargaining power is weak to those where it is
greater.

It is not clear whether inflation increases or decreases the
actual ratio of the national product that goes into investment.
This will depend, in part, on whether or not investment
goods offer greater 'protection' against inflation than non-
investment goods. There are no clear *a priori* statements that
can be made in this area. Further, the empirical evidence does
not allow us to draw any conclusions. The few experiences of
runaway inflation that are well documented are not consistent with growth; if anything, runaway inflation in those
cases depressed the growth level of the economies involved.
In general, unpredictable inflation rates are likely to siphon
off scarce entrepreneurial talents into speculative activities
and away from normal entrepreneurial activities. Relatively
large middlemen are likely to play a significant role in inflation if they are of a type that can easily move from markets
in which their bargaining power is weak to markets in which
it is relatively strong. It is to be hoped that these ideas,
general as they are, are useful in that they suggest research
areas which may lead to an improved understanding of inflationary processes and their consequences.

Our basic analysis began with the concept that all labour
contracts are incomplete. The *complete* part of labour contracts usually involves the price of labour time but not the
actual effort put forth by labour. The concept of labour is
used in the broadest sense to include all members of firms
irrespective of position. Since effort is part of the incomplete portion of labour contracts, this implies that effort, in
terms of pace, quality of work, or activities chosen, is a
variable – it implies some discretionary power on the part of

the individual hired. Hence, firms cannot control all the elements involved that determine the costs of production.

A system of incomplete contracts works for a variety of reasons. Frequently there are some constraints that induce individuals to put forth at least a minimum amount of effort, but beyond the minimum discretion exists. Also, and more important, high costs as a consequence of low effort levels are frequently passed on as higher prices to consumers in industries which are usually imperfectly competitive, This, in part, explains the very frequent use of cost-plus systems of pricing. The reason costs can be passed on is due, in part, to the fact that consumers are frequently in a weak bargaining position and hence cannot bargain actively for the price of commodities; i.e. they face 'take it or leave it' offers. Many sellers, as a consequence of a variety of influences, including elements of imperfect competition and monopolistic competition, frequently possess some discretionary pricing power. In addition, inert areas on the consumer's side enable some sellers to increase prices to some degree with relatively little fear of significant decreases in demand. Producers are frequently in a stronger bargaining position than consumers. This situation allows increases in X-inefficiency on the part of firms to be passed on as higher costs to consumers.

We have also argued that effort level discretion may lead to X-inefficiency. X-inefficiency, in itself, is an element which may contribute to inflation since it increases costs, which in turn leads to the imposition of these costs on others, who are relatively weak in those markets through which the commodities involved have their impact. In a sense we may view X-inefficiency as a way in which incomplete labour contracts can contribute to inflation. Since there is discretion with respect to effort, if the effort level declines and the price of labour per unit of time remains the same, then the effort cost of labour rises. As a result, this becomes part of the cost-push phenomena of building up inflationary pressure. In conventional economic analysis this element is not taken into account, since effort is not viewed as a discretionary variable within the system. Unless we take this into account, we can see that this will become a possible source of inflation which works its way through the system via the multi-bargaining position transmission belt. We have considered in an earlier chapter the network under which economic actors operate in many markets, and each actor who is relatively strong in at least one market will pass on, in his relatively strong market, higher prices imposed on him in weak markets. This last forms a transmission belt for the inflation phenomenon. Of course, those who are weak in all markets are forced to absorb the impact of inflation.

In considering the form which bargaining takes, we placed considerable emphasis on 'take it or leave it' offers in contrast to negotiated bargaining. We saw that where sellers are relatively strong compared to buyers, that this frequently results in the 'take it or leave it' offer as a means of a bargaining. This allows for the creation of inflationary pressures in ways in which negotiated bargaining would not as readily permit. This is especially true with respect to the process we may view as creeping inflation, in the sense that 'take it or leave it' offers, combined with inert areas for consumers, allow relatively resistance-free inflation for relatively long periods. In addition, 'take it or leave it' offers combined with the multi-position bargaining structure that transmits higher prices contributes to the inflationary process. Since those weak in 'take it or leave it' offers may be strong in other markets, they can make up for the losses in weak markets. Of course, those who are weak in *all* markets lose in the process. We have argued that a variety of forces contribute to prevent runaway inflation. In part, the force of inertia leads to somewhat less inflation than would otherwise be the case. In addition, movements of economic actors away from weak markets towards markets in which they are stronger operates as a brake against runaway inflation. This is entirely apart from the governmental budgetary and central bank policies, which may also operate as a brake on runaway inflation.

We have emphasised the inflation transmission chain. Those responsible for the inflationary spark (say a decrease in X-efficiency) are able to avoid the penalty of the impact on costs if they are relatively strong in some market within which they can transfer the impact. Thus, such transfers take place until they hit someone relatively weak in all markets who is forced to bear the brunt of the final impact. 'Take it or leave it' offers enable those who are relatively strong in a market to transmit the impact with very little effect on them or protest from those on whom it falls. Resistance to the impact would manifest itself much more clearly if buyers did not have to respond to 'take it or leave it' offers, but had the option to engage in bargaining negotiations. It is of interest to note a possible asymmetry between the effects of increasing costs as a result of increasing X-inefficiency, and decreasing costs. We have suggested various ways in which increasing costs lead to higher prices. However, decreasing costs do not necessarily lead to lower prices. Due to inert areas within firms, lower costs may not initially lead to lower prices but rather to increased profits. This in turn may lead to an increased demand for higher wages or prices by the owners of the inputs, which in turn lead to constant or higher input costs. One way this last may work its way through the system is that higher profits may attract entrepreneurs to expand the scale of the industry, which in turn may cause employees to bargain for higher wages, which in turn raises costs per unit. Consequently, this may or may not raise prices depending on the degree to which entrepreneurial activities bid up the prices of inputs. We must keep in mind in all these discussions that costs depend on *both* the price of inputs and on effort levels.

We have argued that in various ways inflation affects the distribution of income, but we emphasised that a significant way in which it affects income distribution is through its impact of those who are especially *vulnerable* to decrease in real income. One reason for emphasising vulnerability is because of some of the technical difficulties of measuring changes in income distribution.

Different definitions and indices of income inequality data lead to different types of measures of inequality. Of greater importance is the fact that we care about inflation because there are losers as a result of inflation. Furthermore we are likely to be more concerned with those who are vulnerable to such losses as against those who are not. Hence, our emphasis on vulnerability as a criterion for assessing the impact of inflation. There is considerable likelihood that in many cases there will be a high correlation between those at the lower end of the income distribution and those vulnerable to the impact of inflation. Hence, the vulnerability criterion is especially significant in connection with our concern with income distributions as such.

On the basis of our review of some of the empirical literature, we found that it is extremely difficult to generalise about the impact of inflation on development. Nevertheless, the ideas that we have developed suggest certain significant questions that we should ask in empirical studies about the impact of inflation on development. It is in this spirit that a variety of speculations about the relationship between inflation, income distribution, and development of LDCs are offered.

Because LDCs are characterised, and indeed defined, by low income *per capita*, they are particular areas where relatively large portions of the population may be vulnerable to reductions in real income. This is unquestionably the case with respect to those in the lower half or lowest third of the income distribution. Consider for a moment the effect of real income changes on food consumption. In most developing countries the nutritional standard is usually adequate in terms of calories *per capita*. This is likely to be true for the average consumer but not for those in the lower half or lowest third of the income distribution. The lower the nutritional standard, the greater the vulnerability for any further reduction in that standard. This is true not only in terms of capacity to carry out useful work. This in turn may lead (in some cases) to vicious circles in which a low nutritional standard makes it difficult for some to put forth sufficient effort to produce enough output to raise the standard. Empirical evidence has also demonstrated that the psychological consequences of a low level of nutrition are frequently more significant than the purely physical effects on health.[1] Low nutrition levels generally lead to a high degree of inertia, lethargy, etc., so that it becomes extremely difficult for such individuals to take advantage of opportunities which may improve their output and consumption levels. It is not necessary to go into great detail about the nature of this process, but clearly such hypotheses are part of the problem of generating *per capita* income growth in developing countries.

Vulnerability to inflation is likely to hold even for those households in the lower portions of income distribution who lag behind in the inflation race. Accumulated savings are likely to be exceedingly low. Thus, vulnerability may even be significant to members of groups for whom inflation does not result in any long-run loss but only in a lag of six months to a year in the catching-up process. For the most part it is these groups who do not have the means, or access to the means, to tide them over adequately until the catching-up process takes place.

One of the usual ways in which people attempt to protect themselves against inflation is to shift the form of their assets so that they retain their real value in face of value changes in current prices. Thus, some individuals will shift into ownership of gold or jewellery or such assets as houses, apartments, etc., whose specific monetary valuations keep up with the overall inflation rate. But all of this requires the ownership of assets to start with. Furthermore they have to be saleable assets. This is unlikely to be true for those whose only assets are essentially their capacity to work, or some minimal amount of land and agricultural equipment used for small-scale farming, or for those who are sharecroppers. Since the asset distribution is likely to be more unequal than the income distribution, and in some sense 'excess assets' are necessary to protect oneself from the vulnerability to inflationary losses, one can see that these general ideas are of special significance for those who earn their livelihood in developing countries.

In some cases the impact of inflation is likely to reduce the level of employment since inflation may stimulate investment in assets that operate as a hedge against inflation, without regard to the degree to which such assets are of an employment-creating nature. In addition we have argued that inflation is likely to shift the limited supply of entrepreneurship away from growth and employment-producing activities and into speculative activities.

To the extent that unemployment is widespread in developing countries, it is important to keep in mind that the means to weathering periods of unemployment is likely to be extremely limited in LDCs. Unemployment insurance, as such, is likely to be unavailable in most instances. Clearly, these factors play a critical role in determining vulnerability.

On the other hand, some LDCs are characterised by a self-contained, nonmarket agricultural sub-sector. To the extent that this sector is large, it is likely to operate as a relative hedge against inflation, since it is uninvolved in the monetary economy. Members of this sub-sector are likely to be found in the lower levels of the income distribution. Hence, the size of this sector must be taken into account in assessing the overall impact of inflation. Generally though, most households in contemporary LDCs are likely to be connected with the monetised sector to some degree, and in these cases our emphasis on relative multi-position bargaining power is of significance in assessing the impact of inflation on vulnerability.

II. Remarks on Policy Implications

It is extremely difficult to indicate desirable and practical policies which are anti-inflationary in the context of developing countries. This becomes especially true if we emphasise *practical* policies, that is, policies that are at all likely to be adopted by political authorities. The reason for this is that inflation is a process that is very much involved in the inter-action between economic and political considerations. A policy is likely to make some groups worse off and other groups better off. By the same token it is important to note that having no policy (i.e. doing nothing) will also make some groups better off and other groups worse off — on the average. In addition to the political constraints of carrying out anti-inflation policies, there are also subtle welfare considerations involved. Namely, any policy which is likely to redistribute income, as well as having other effects, implies certain welfare presumptions from the outset. Hence, what we could consider are sets of possible policies that flow from the previous chapters, but we cannot develop *a priori* policies which recommend themselves simply on the basis of the considerations reviewed in this volume. The reason for this should be self-evident. This study has been an exercise in positive economics. No attempt has been made to develop a counterpart set of welfare postulates which would be acceptable by all. Most likely no such set exists.

Traditionally, welfare economics is not suitable because its most vulnerable point is precisely the issue of income redistribution. Thus very little could be suggested which would lead to what economists could call Pareto-superior situations. That is, there are almost no policies which would guarantee to make everyone better off and no-one worse off. Also, even if there were such policies, making some individuals better off without making anybody worse off implies a different income distribution. As a consequence, once our main concern is income distribution as such, we can see that traditional welfare economics is not suitable to handle these problems. Nevertheless, one could suggest some possible policies that should be put on the agenda for *consideration* for any programme concerned with handling the impact of inflation in developing countries.

One surprising result (at least to the author) which occurred as a by-product of the work on this study, is the discovery that no systematic work has been done on who gains and who loses in the inflationary process. Thus, there exists a type of knowledge of an empirical sort which could be carried out in principle and which has not been carried out. Clearly, work of this kind is absolutely necessary prior to selecting rational anti-inflationary policies. Frequently policies have to be chosen with insufficient knowledge because the practical exigencies of the situation require such choices. Nevertheless, wherever time and resources allow, it would seem to be useful to try to determine in a systematic way who gains and who loses in inflation. Two types of concerns are involved. On the one hand one could attempt to determine who gains and who loses according to the standard occupational categories. However, it would also be desirable to get some idea about gains and losses within each occupational category. Second, it would be especially useful in determining policy to attempt to assess which group in the population are especially vulnerable to the types of losses that occur during inflation. We have already argued in the first chapter that, despite difficulties in making statements about the desirability of different types of income distribution, it is probably easier to make statements about the degrees of vulnerability, or at least the category of extreme vulnerability, and to base policies so that those groups who are extremely vulnerable are either put in positions where they are less likely to suffer from inflation, or compensated for inflationary losses. It is likely that the greatest concern would be for those whose vulnerability is to the maintenance of a subsistence standard of consumption, or a very low relative standard, given the average consumption level in the economy. There are others for whom vulnerability may be the customary standard. Whatever criteria we establish for caring about different types of vulnerability, it would seem desirable to attempt assessments of the degree of vulnerability with respect to inflation. Once we assess the degree of vulnerability, we are in a position to establish some priorities with respect to judging policies in terms of the extent to which a decrease in vulnerability of various groups, are in terms of priorities initially chosen.

In assessing the various anti-inflationary policies it seems natural to start with the normal *macro* policies used by governments; that is, (i) controlling the money or credit supply, and (ii) the budgetary policies of government. Clearly, anything governments can do to reduce the rates of inflation will also reduce the vulnerability to inflation. Nevertheless, in considering such policies, the various vulnerabilities and income distribution impacts must be taken into account. For instance, one way of controlling the quantity of credit is for the central government and the central bank to increase interest rates. To the extent that interest rates influence capital accumulation and the rate of expansion of different industries, they are likely to affect different industries differently, and monopolies differently form competitive industries. Monopolies are usually less vulnerable to cost increases. The outcome with respect to income distribution is likely to be quite complex since the relative demand elasticities for the products involved have to be considered, as well as the degree to which lower income individuals depend on employment in expanding, as against nonexpanding industries. An additional factor is likely to be the relative bargaining power of lower income employees in expanding versus nonexpanding industries. This is not the place to trace the entire constellation of possible consequences that can occur on the basis of different elasticities of demand, different price policies pursued, and different constellations of multi-position bargaining power. It should be clear on the basis of our analysis that such a policy is unlikely to be neutral with respect to its impact on income distribution, and on those who are vulnerable to real income changes.

To the extent that lower income groups are predominantly borrowers and rent payers, they may gain through inflation if their interest payments and rents are in initial money values. Nevertheless the distribution of debts and the nature of contracts introduces complications – so that this aspect must be assessed empirically on a case-by-case basis. The main point of these remarks is to alert the reader to the fact that normal anti-inflationary policies should be reconsidered in terms of the vulnerability criteria developed in Chapter 1.

A general policy that follows from the previous chapters is for the government involved to work out a system of transfer payments from those who gain most (in *net* terms) by inflation to those who are net losers and who are most vulnerable to the impact of inflation. Clearly, for such a policy to be well designed and carried out, the type of research suggested in previous paragraphs (on the gains and losses from inflation) would be a necessary prelude. There are various specific forms such a policy could take. Details would have to depend on specific circumstances and practicalities in specific contexts.

One possibility is an inflation tax. If firms in a country kept good accounting records, then it might be possible on the basis of such records to separate that portion of the firm's income earned on the basis of previous prices, as against that portion which reflects inflationary *increases* in prices of outputs and inputs. If such records were readily available and administrative costs were not too high, it would be possible to impose inflation-earnings taxes at the same time that government bureaus levied income taxes, profit taxes or other business taxes. The proceeds could then be used to reimburse those who lose by inflation and are vulnerable to its impact.

Unfortunately, for many developing countries the accounting records are unlikely to be sufficiently developed, and the administrative cost of enforcement too high, to impose a system of taxes and subsidies on the same basis that income taxes are levied and collected in developed countries. Nevertheless, it may be possible to assess gains and losses from inflation for extreme cases. In other words, within some level of inflation gains and losses, say up to some predetermined percentage of the average inflation rate in either direction, no

levies would be made or subsidies granted. Errors in calculation could easily equal the smaller variations in gains and
losses. But in more extreme cases attempts may be made to
assess gains and losses, and to levy taxes and grant subsidies.

Where the administrative set-up does not allow for any
type of explicit inflation-earnings taxes, it may nevertheless
be desirable to offer subsidies to those most vulnerable to
inflation out of general governmental revenue. Such an
approach faces a number of difficulties. First, unless the
subsidies are balanced by tax increases, this in itself will have
an inflationary effect. Furthermore, increased taxes may be
levied inadvertently on the losers from the inflationary process, as well as on those who gain. Thus we see that there are
inherent difficulties in subsidising those vulnerable to inflationary losses, unless we can determine who receives inflationary gains. Nevertheless, in a practical situation, one may
have to balance the risks of achieving greater inequities
against the gain from creating a more equitable situation
through subsidising those who are most vulnerable.

Almost all policies that come to mind depend on being
able to assess those responsible for inflation and those who
achieve inflationary gains, not only in the private sector but
also in and by governmental units and organs. In most developing countries, the government is engaged in offering
favours and privileges to various firms, be they private or
public. The most common ways in which favours are dis-
pensed are through the issuance of import licences, and
offering tax benefits and remissions, in order to encourage
firms to undertake various types of economic activities. One
criterion that could be used in determining who gets licences
or tax remissions is the degree of inflationary pressure
created by the firm in the past. Of course it need not be the
only criterion. Those firms that influence inflation less would
be offered more points for licences or tax benefits than those
who influence inflation to a greater degree.

To the extent that increasing X-inefficiency is an inflationary force, systems of taxes or subsidies which reward firms

that increase labour productivity, without increasing prices, could be part of a general policy package which favours maintaining or increasing the degree of X-efficiency in the economy. Along the same lines, similar means may be used to urge firms and farms to use consulting services which would increase X-efficiency. Such consulting services (or agriculture extension services) may come from either the private or public sector. In addition, wage payment formulas which maintain the *real* wages of the most vulnerable employees are likely to be helpful. To some degree governments may be in a position to develop policies and reward mechanisms which induce firms to adopt such formulas. A possible difficulty that may arise in this connection is that such formulas may, while helping the more vulnerable members of the work-force, develop incentives so that they reduce their X-efficiency. While this need not occur, it is a factor that has to be considered in designing policies which favour the real-wage maintenance of vulnerable groups.

A policy likely to be most helpful in reducing vulnerability is to increase the human capital (through education, on-the-job training, etc.) of the less skilled members of the work-force. This is likely to have at least two desirable conse-quences: it increases the earning potential of lower income individuals. Possibly of equal importance, it may provide such individuals with a greater degree of mobility between occupa-tions so that they can move out of occupations where they are vulnerable to inflation and into those where their vulner-ability is less. The normal cautionary remarks in this area hold in the sense that some forms of education, which in theory increase human capital, may in fact increase the supply of educated labour in areas where no counterpart jobs are available. This says nothing more than that policies of this kind must take employment potential into account. One lesson that the history of many developing countries teaches is that the supply of educated manpower does not create its own demand.

A relatively sensitive policy area that should be considered is population policies. Policies which permit households to control their fertility as much as they wish to can be defended purely on the desirability of maximising individual choice. Providing the means to help individuals to determine child spacing and family size increases a household's capacity to cope with its social and economic environment. Such policies are probably neutral with respect to reducing income inequality in the shorter run. The exact outcome depends on which elements of income respond most to such options and policies. However, in terms of reducing vulnerability, to the extent that the lower half of the income distribution takes advantage of services provided by such policies, it is likely to reduce the burden of dependency of families in the lower income levels and hence reduce their vulnerability. In any event it would seem one could argue that low income groups should at least have the choice to reduce vulnerability to income fluctuations, even if not all of them take advantage of the opportunities offered.

One of the most difficult aspects of the problem is the relationship between inflation and unemployment. It is certainly possible for those who raise prices to do so to a degree where they reduce the quantities demand of consumption goods, or to increase the credit needed to maintain a given rate of investment beyond credit availability so that unemployment increases. What happens will depend on a variety of elasticities that take into account the rate of responsiveness of entrepreneurs to increased opportunities, increased money demand, and/or demand for credit, the responsiveness of savers to increased interest rates, and so on. A variety of models could be developed which would indicate under what constellation of circumstances inflation would be employment-creating, as against those under which it would depress employment. We cannot go into the possibilities here. However, we can suggest that one aspect to be considered is the degree to which inflation fosters or induces a reduction of labour-intensive capital. To the extent that such capital operates as a hedge against inflation, if it is readily saleable, it is likely that the type of equipment used in *developed* economies will be favoured in LDCs over capital goods especially suited to the relative scarcities of capital and labour in developing countries. As a result, in some industries there is likely to be a labour-saving bias in equipment utilised. From this point of view it would appear to be desirable for governments to use their tax or licensing powers to foster more labour-intensive means of production — especially where more labour-intensive methods increase the demand for labour amongst the more vulnerable households.

At this stage of our analysis, especially given the paucity of empirical data available, we can only limit ourselves to statements of a suggestive nature. Many of the ideas considered are too new, and factual evidence too sparse, to do much else. Nevertheless, we hope that the analysis presented will help to raise empirical and policy considerations that otherwise would not be considered in examining the impact of inflation on income distribution and employment, in the context of economic development.

Notes

1. See Ancel Keys, *The Biology of Starvation* (University of Minn. Press, Minnesota, 1950) (2 vols.).

INDEX